The Light You Can Reach

Practical Tools for Building a Bridge Out of the Dark

Angie G. Ford

Sunflower Phoenix Publishing

ISBN: 979-8-9959413-5-4

Published by Sunflower Phoenix Publishing

This book is not a substitute for professional medical advice, diagnosis, therapy, crisis care, or treatment. If you are in crisis, please call or text 988 in the United States, contact emergency services, go to the nearest emergency room, or reach for a qualified mental health professional or safe person who can be with you now.

Table of Contents

For anyone who is tired of being told to try harder when even breathing already feels like work.

A Note Before We Begin

This book is not a substitute for medical care, therapy, crisis support, or the guidance of a qualified mental health professional.

It is a companion.

It is a small book of tools for the person who already knows the dark, the person who has already felt the weight of the blanket, the concrete in the body, the voice in the room, the strange ache of the light when it breaks through too suddenly.

If you are in immediate danger, or if you may hurt yourself, please stop reading and reach for another human being right now. In the United States, you can call or text 988 to reach the Suicide & Crisis Lifeline. You do not have to explain your whole life. You only have to say enough to let someone stand between you and the dark for this moment.

A book can sit with you.

A book can give language.

A book can offer a tool.

But when the dark is too heavy, you need a person.

Please let a person help you stay.

Introduction: The Bridge Starts Small

In the first book, we sat in the dark together.

We did not rush toward the light. We did not pretend the dark was just sadness. We did not call the mask weakness. We did not tell the body to hurry up and become light again. We did not demand gratitude from a nervous system that could barely breathe.

We named things.

We named the house of depression.

We named the strange comfort of the dark.

We named the mask.

We named the splinter of light.

We named the voice that sounds like you but is not telling the truth.

We named the exhaustion of being helped by people whose love sometimes feels like pressure.

We named the body that feels like concrete, the vacuum in the chest, the shower that is not just a shower, and the candle that does not have to become the sun.

That naming mattered.

Sometimes the first form of relief is not a solution. Sometimes the first form of relief is having someone describe the room you have been trapped in so accurately that you finally stop wondering if you invented it.

Book 1 was not an action plan.

It was never meant to be.

It was a hand on the floor beside you. It was someone saying, I know this place. You are not the only one here.

This book is different.

This book is an action plan.

But not the kind that shouts at you.

Not the kind that tells you to overhaul your life, fix your mindset, build a morning routine, become disciplined, glow from the inside, drink more water, go for a run, forgive everyone, write a gratitude list, and reinvent yourself by Monday.

That is not the kind of action plan a person in the dark can carry.

That kind of plan becomes another weight.

This book is made of smaller things.

It is made of tools that can fit in a trembling hand.

It is made for the person who may not have hope today, but might have ten seconds of attention.

It is made for the person who cannot think about recovery, but might be able to name one thought as a voice.

It is made for the person who cannot build a whole bridge, but might be able to lay one board across the dark.

These tools are not theory to me.

They are small things that helped real people stay, breathe, and begin again.

Not all at once.

Not cleanly.

Not without falling back into the dark sometimes.

But slowly, one board at a time, they helped make a way where there had not been one before.

We are not going to ask you to become the sun.

We are not even going to ask you to walk toward the sun.

We are going to begin with what is reachable.

A pause.

A breath.

A gap.

A shower with soap.

Clean clothes, if you can.

The bed pulled straight, if you have enough left.

Not because these things fix depression.

Because they give the day a beginning.

And sometimes a beginning is the first clean signal the dark cannot easily erase.

From there, we will keep building.

We will make a small room in your mind where the voice does not get to hold the only chair.

We will learn how to survive the good days without turning them into a contract.

We will learn how to survive the days when the tools fail, because they will fail sometimes, and that will not mean you failed.

We will learn how to notice color when it returns slowly, cautiously, unevenly, like it is not sure you are ready to see it yet.

These are not magic tricks.

They are not cures.

They are not proof that you should be better by now.

They are tools.

A tool does not shame you for needing it.

A bridge does not accuse you because the gap exists.

A candle does not demand that you become daylight.

It only gives you enough light to see the next inch.

That is what we are doing here.

Not the whole road.

Not the whole future.

Just the next inch.

If Book 1 said, you are not alone in this room, Book 2 says, while we are here, let me show you where the matches are.

You do not have to use every tool.

You do not have to use them perfectly.

You do not have to feel inspired by them.

You can be skeptical. You can be exhausted. You can be angry that you need tools at all. You can read this book from the same bed, under the same blanket, with the same heaviness in your limbs.

Nothing about that disqualifies you.

We will begin gently.

We will return to what we already named.

And then, one small piece at a time, we will learn what to do when the light hurts.

For Today

You do not have to build the whole bridge today.

You only have to believe that one small board might be enough to start.

Chapter 1: The Splinter Pause

When the Light Finds the Tender Place

There is a reason we have to begin here.

Not with motivation.

Not with discipline.

Not with a list of healthy habits taped to the refrigerator.

We have to begin with the splinter.

Because when you are deep in the dark, the first thing that reaches you may not feel like hope.

It may feel like pain.

You might be walking through a grocery store, moving slowly under the fluorescent lights, trying to remember why you came in. You are standing in the cereal aisle, holding the cart with both hands because even the cart feels like something you are using to stay upright.

Then you hear a child laughing two aisles over.

It is a full laugh.

A real laugh.

The kind of laugh that has no self-consciousness in it. The kind that tumbles out before the mind has time to manage it.

For half a second, something in you responds.

Not much.

Just a tiny flicker.

A memory of what it felt like when sound could reach you without hurting. A memory of being in the world without calculating every movement. A memory of laughter as something possible.

And then the pain comes.

It arrives so quickly it can feel like punishment.

The warmth cracks open the numbness, and behind it comes the ache. The light shows you the distance between that child's laughter and the vacuum in your chest. It shows you what seems to belong to other people and not to you. It shows you the part of the world still moving while you feel pinned under something heavy and invisible.

For a moment, the dark is not just dark.

It has contrast.

And contrast hurts.

That is the splinter.

Book 1 named it.

This book is going to teach you how to pause with it.

Not because pausing will make it stop hurting immediately.

Not because pausing will turn the grocery aisle into a spiritual awakening.

Not because you are supposed to become grateful for the pain.

The Splinter Pause is not a way to force the light to feel good.

It is a way to keep the pain of the light from becoming a whole story about your life.

That distinction matters.

Because the splinter itself may be painful, but what often happens next can be even heavier.

The splinter arrives.

You feel the contrast.

And then the voice starts building a case.

It says, See? You cannot even handle a child laughing.

It says, Other people get to live. You just watch.

It says, This is proof that joy is gone for good.

It says, You are too broken for the world now.

The original pain may have lasted three seconds.

The story can last all day.

The Splinter Pause is the tiny space we create before the story takes over.

It is not a cure.

It is not a command to be positive.

It is a hand on the door before the voice storms into the room.

20

The Moment Before the Verdict

Depression loves a verdict.

It does not want a moment to remain a moment. It wants every moment to become evidence.

If you cannot answer a text, depression calls it proof that you are a bad friend.

If you cannot get out of bed, depression calls it proof that you are lazy.

If you feel pain when the light breaks through, depression calls it proof that hope is dangerous.

This is how the dark turns small experiences into permanent sentences.

It takes something brief and turns it into forever.

The Splinter Pause interrupts that process.

It gives you one small practice before the verdict forms.

The practice is simple on purpose.

When the splinter of light hurts, you say to yourself:

This is a splinter of light.

Then you say:

It hurts because I am tender, not because I am hopeless.

That is all.

You do not have to believe it completely.

You do not have to feel calm.

You do not have to stop crying in the cereal aisle.

You do not have to turn the moment into a lesson.

You only have to place one sentence between the pain and the verdict.

This is a splinter of light.

It hurts because I am tender, not because I am hopeless.

That sentence is a small board across the gap.

It may not hold your whole weight yet.

That is okay.

It is still a board.

Why the Pause Has to Be Small

A person who is not depressed may hear the word pause and imagine something peaceful.

They may imagine closing their eyes, taking a deep breath, placing both hands over the heart, and entering a calm state of self-awareness.

That is lovely.

It is also not always available in the dark.

When depression has drained the body and narrowed the mind, even a pause can feel like too much. Asking yourself to process an emotion, regulate your nervous system, challenge a thought, practice gratitude, and choose a healthier response may be more than you can carry.

So we are not going to begin there.

The Splinter Pause is not a full emotional exercise.

It is a recognition.

Recognition is smaller than transformation.

Recognition says, I see what is happening.

That is enough for the first step.

You see the couple laughing together on the sidewalk.

The warmth arrives.

The ache follows.

The voice begins moving toward its verdict.

And somewhere in that small, painful space, you name it.

This is a splinter.

You do not have to do anything heroic after that.

You can look away.

You can go home.

You can sit in the car for ten minutes before turning the key.

You can cry.

You can rest.

The goal is not to hold onto the light.

The goal is only to stop the darkness from using the light as a weapon against you.

The Five Small Parts of the Splinter Pause

If you have enough steadiness to practice the full version, the Splinter Pause has five small parts.

They are not steps in the productivity sense.

They are not a checklist you have to complete correctly.

They are more like five stones across a shallow stream. You may use all of them. You may only reach the first one. Some days, the first one will be enough.

The first stone is Name It.

You say:

This is a splinter of light.

Not, I am falling apart.

Not, I cannot handle joy.

Not, This proves I will never get better.

Just:

This is a splinter of light.

Naming matters because unnamed pain expands. It fills the whole room. Once it has a name, it becomes something you are experiencing, not the entirety of who you are.

The second stone is Locate It.

You ask:

Where did it hurt?

Maybe it hurt in your chest.

Maybe it hit your throat.

Maybe your stomach dropped.

Maybe your eyes burned.

Maybe your whole body went numb.

You are not asking this so you can analyze the pain. You are asking so your mind does not immediately turn the pain into a life sentence.

The body speaks in sensation before the mind speaks in verdicts.

If you can notice the sensation, even briefly, you may have one small moment before the story takes over.

The third stone is Separate It.

You say:

This hurts because I am in the dark. This does not mean the light is gone forever.

This matters.

The pain of contrast can trick you into believing that joy itself is the enemy. It can make you want to avoid every bright thing because the drop afterward feels unbearable.

Avoiding the light may make sense for survival sometimes.

You are allowed to protect your eyes.

But the Splinter Pause helps you remember that the pain is not proof that light is impossible. It is proof that the place it touched is tender.

Tender is not hopeless.

Tender is injured.

Tender can be protected.

Tender can be given time.

The fourth stone is Soften the Story.

You say:

I do not have to turn this moment into a prophecy.

This may be the most important sentence in the whole practice.

A prophecy says, This is how it will always be.

A prophecy says, I felt pain when I saw happiness, so happiness will always hurt.

A prophecy says, The dark came back after the light, so the light was a trick.

But you do not have to let one moment predict the rest of your life.

You are allowed to let it be one moment.

A sharp one.

A painful one.

A real one.

But still one moment.

The fifth stone is Return Gently.

You ask:

What is the kindest next inch?

Not the next mile.

Not the next hour.

Not the plan for recovery.

The next inch.

Maybe the kindest next inch is leaving the room.

Maybe it is drinking water.

Maybe it is putting your phone down.

Maybe it is taking a shower later and sending one clean signal.

Maybe it is going back to bed without calling yourself weak.

Maybe it is texting someone:

The dark is loud today. Can you sit with me for a minute?

The point is not to make the splinter useful.

The point is to make the moment survivable.

When You Cannot Do All Five

There will be days when five stones are too many.

There will be days when the splinter hits and you cannot name it until hours later.

There will be days when the pain turns into a story before you even realize what happened.

There will be days when you avoid the light completely because you simply cannot handle one more contrast.

This does not mean you failed the tool.

It means you are human, and the dark is heavy.

A tool is not a test.

A tool is something you can pick up when your hand is able to close around it.

If you cannot do the full Splinter Pause, use the smallest version.

Just say:

Splinter.

That one word can be enough.

You see an old photograph of yourself smiling.

The grief hits.

You whisper:

Splinter.

You hear music you used to love.

For two seconds, it reaches you, and then the ache comes behind it.

You whisper:

Splinter.

You watch someone you love enjoy a simple moment, and instead of feeling only warmth, you feel the terrible distance between their ease and your exhaustion.

You whisper:

Splinter.

One word.

One label.

One tiny interruption.

It may not make you feel better.

But it may help you feel less confused by the pain.

Less ashamed of it.

Less convinced that it means something terrible about you.

That matters.

The Splinter Is Not the Enemy

It is tempting to hate the splinter.

Of course it is.

Anything that hurts becomes something we want to avoid.

But the splinter is complicated.

It hurts because light is entering a place that has been dark for a long time. It hurts because something in you is still capable of responding. It hurts because the numbness is not complete.

That does not make the pain beautiful.

We do not need to romanticize it.

Pain is pain.

But the splinter is not proof that you are ruined.

It is proof that some part of you is still reachable.

Even if the light only reaches you as ache.

Even if warmth feels like grief.

Even if hope feels sharp.

Something in you still knows the difference between darkness and light.

That knowing may feel unbearable right now.

But it is not nothing.

It is a signal.

A painful one.

A small one.

A signal all the same.

The Splinter Pause does not ask you to celebrate that signal.

It only asks you not to let depression turn it into an accusation.

You are not weak because the light hurts.

You are not ungrateful because joy is painful to witness.

You are not broken because contrast knocks the breath out of you.

You are tender where the light is touching.

That is all we have to know for today.

Practicing After the Moment Has Passed

Sometimes you will not catch the splinter when it happens.

You will only understand it afterward.

That still counts.

You may come home from dinner with friends and collapse on the bed, suddenly full of grief, shame, and exhaustion. At the restaurant, everyone laughed. The candles were lit. The food smelled good. Someone told a story, and for a few minutes, you almost felt present.

Then you got home, and the dark returned harder than before.

The voice began its work.

It told you the good moment was fake.

It told you that you were pretending.

It told you that if you were really getting better, you would not have crashed afterward.

Hours later, maybe with your coat still on, maybe with the room still dark, you can practice the pause retroactively.

You can say:

That was a splinter of light.

It hurt afterward because the contrast was intense.

The crash does not erase the moment.

The moment does not obligate me to be better tomorrow.

This matters because depression loves to rewrite good moments after they happen.

It says the crash invalidates the light.

But the crash does not erase the candle.

It only means the candle did not light the whole forest.

We already knew it would not.

A candle is still a candle.

A moment is still a moment.

A laugh is still a laugh, even if you cried afterward.

The Splinter Pause can help you protect those moments from being stolen completely by what came next.

Not preserved perfectly.

Not framed as progress.

Just protected enough that depression does not get to call them lies.

What to Do With the Pain

The hardest question is always this:

What do I do with the pain once I have named it?

Sometimes the honest answer is nothing.

You let it be there.

You let the ache exist without forcing it to become useful.

You do not have to transform every hurt into wisdom.

You do not have to mine every painful moment for meaning.

Some pain is just pain.

But if you have a little steadiness, you can give the pain somewhere to go.

You can put a hand on your chest and say:

This is tender.

You can breathe once, not deeply, not perfectly, just once with awareness.

You can step outside for sixty seconds and let the air touch your face.

You can wash your hands with soap and let that be your clean signal for the hour.

You can write one sentence on a scrap of paper:

The light hurt today, but it did reach me.

Then you can stop.

Stopping is part of the tool.

This is where many action plans become dangerous. They turn one small practice into a doorway that opens onto twenty more demands. They say, Now that you have noticed the splinter, journal for thirty minutes, call a friend, go for a walk, clean the kitchen, and make a plan.

No.

Not here.

Here, you are allowed to stop after the pause.

You are allowed to let the practice be complete.

You are allowed to return to the blanket, the bed, the quiet room, the low light.

The Splinter Pause is a closed loop.

You named it.

You softened the story.

You chose the kindest next inch, even if that inch was rest.

That is enough.

When the Splinter Is Too Sharp

There may be times when the splinter of light does not feel small.

It may tear through you.

A memory may hit with such force that you cannot breathe around it.

A photograph, a song, a holiday, a child's laugh, a friend's happiness, an ordinary morning full of birdsong may open something so painful that the ground disappears under you.

If that happens, do not try to practice alone if being alone feels unsafe.

If the voice begins telling you that you cannot stay, that people would be better without you, that the pain proves you should disappear, this is no longer a private practice moment.

This is a reach-for-help moment.

Call or text 988 if you are in the United States and might hurt yourself.

Tell someone:

The voice is loud. I should not be alone right now.

You do not have to make it eloquent.

You do not have to explain the whole story.

You do not have to prove that your pain is serious enough.

If the dark is pulling you toward danger, another human being needs to know.

The tools in this book are for the moments when tools can help.

They are not meant to replace rescue.

Let yourself be rescued when rescue is what is needed.

That, too, is a tool.

That, too, is survival.

The First Board of the Bridge

The Splinter Pause is the first board of the bridge because it teaches a skill you will need again and again.

It teaches you to notice the moment before depression turns pain into identity.

It teaches you to place a little space between what happened and what the voice says it means.

It teaches you that a sharp feeling does not have to become a permanent verdict.

This is the beginning of many things.

It will help when we talk about the Voice Gap.

It will help when we talk about One Clean Signal.

It will help when we talk about good days, because good days can be their own kind of splinter. They can bring relief, but they can also bring fear.

Fear that the relief will leave.

Fear that people will expect too much now.

Fear that if the darkness returns, it will mean the good day was a lie.

The Splinter Pause will help there, too.

For now, we are starting small.

The next time the light hurts, if you can, do not rush to explain it.

Do not let the voice turn it into a prophecy.

Do not shame yourself for flinching.

Just name it.

This is a splinter of light.

It hurts because I am tender, not because I am hopeless.

Then ask for the kindest next inch.

That may be all you can do.

That may be plenty.

For Today

When the light hurts, you do not have to turn the pain into a prophecy.

You can name it.

You can breathe once.

You can choose the kindest next inch.

Splinter.

That may be enough for today.

Chapter 2: The Voice Gap

When the Lie Sounds Like You

There is a voice that can become so familiar you stop hearing it as a voice.

It does not always sound dramatic.

It does not always arrive like an enemy.

Sometimes it sounds calm.

Sometimes it sounds practical.

Sometimes it sounds like the most honest thing in the room.

You wake up, and the first thought is already waiting.

I cannot do this today.

Not as a feeling.

As a fact.

You look at the message you have not answered, and the voice says:

You are a terrible friend.

You see the dishes in the sink, the laundry in the basket, the unopened mail on the table, and the voice says:

This is what you are now.

You hear someone laugh in the other room, and the voice says:

They would be lighter without you.

That last one matters.

If the voice ever tells you that people would be better without you, that you should disappear, that you should hurt yourself, or that you cannot stay alive, please do not treat that as a private thought you have to manage alone.

That is a reach-for-help moment.

If you are in the United States and you may hurt yourself, call or text 988. If you are in immediate danger, contact emergency services or get to another human being now.

You do not have to explain it perfectly.

You can say:

The voice is loud, and I should not be alone.

That is enough to begin.

The tools in this book are for the moments when tools can help.

They are not meant to replace rescue.

And sometimes rescue is the tool.

For the moments when the voice is painful but not pulling you into immediate danger, we are going to learn the second board of the bridge.

The Voice Gap.

Book 1 named the awful strangeness of depression speaking in your own voice. It named the way a thought can arrive wearing your face, using your tone, sounding like your private wisdom, even when it is not telling the truth.

That is one of the cruelest parts.

If the dark spoke in a voice you did not recognize, you might reject it more easily.

If it sounded like a stranger standing in your kitchen, saying terrible things about you, you might know to step away.

But depression often sounds like you.

It uses your memories.

It uses your shame.

It uses your exhaustion.

It uses the evidence lying around the room.

The unread messages.

The unwashed hair.

The days you have lost.

The promises you meant to keep.

The good people you do not have energy to answer.

Then it builds a case and calls the case clarity.

The Voice Gap is not a way to argue with that voice until you win.

Most days, you will not win an argument with the dark by force.

The Voice Gap is smaller than that.

It is the space between hearing the thought and obeying it.

It is the breath between the sentence and the verdict.

It is the quiet second where you say:

That is the voice. I do not have to answer it yet.

Not forever.

Not with perfect confidence.

Just yet.

That one word can save you from believing too quickly.

Yet.

The Thought and the Truth

A thought can feel true without being the whole truth.

That is hard to remember when depression is loud.

The voice does not usually say, Here is one possible interpretation of your current emotional state.

It says, This is who you are.

It says, This is how it will always be.

It says, Everyone is tired of you.

It says, You ruin things.

It says, There is no point in trying.

It does not speak with question marks.

It speaks with periods.

That is one way you can begin to recognize it.

Depression loves a final sentence.

It does not leave room for tenderness, timing, context, illness, exhaustion, or the ordinary fact that human beings are allowed to have days when they cannot hold everything.

The Voice Gap begins by noticing the shape of the sentence.

Is it absolute?

Is it cruel?

Is it permanent?

Is it pretending to know the future?

Is it using one hard moment as proof of your whole identity?

If so, you do not have to call it truth right away.

You can call it the voice.

This is not about pretending everything is fine.

If there are dishes in the sink, there are dishes in the sink.

If you have not answered the message, you have not answered the message.

If you stayed in bed all day, that happened.

The Voice Gap does not ask you to deny reality.

It asks you to separate reality from the punishment attached to it.

Reality says, There are dishes in the sink.

The voice says, You are disgusting.

Reality says, I have not answered that message.

The voice says, I am a terrible friend and everyone should leave me.

Reality says, Today is very hard.

The voice says, Every day will be this hard forever.

The gap lives between those sentences.

That is where we begin.

The Core Sentence

The smallest version of this tool is one sentence.

That is the voice. I do not have to answer it yet.

You do not have to say it out loud.

You can, if it helps.

You can whisper it into the blanket.

You can write it on a sticky note.

You can type it into your phone.

You can think only the first half if the whole sentence is too much.

The voice.

That can be enough.

The point is not to make the thought vanish.

The point is to stop fusing with it so completely that it becomes your only reality.

When a thought and your identity become glued together, there is no room to breathe. The thought says, I am worthless, and before you even know what happened, you are no longer having a thought.

You are worthless.

The sentence has swallowed you.

The Voice Gap gently peels the sentence back from your skin.

Not all the way.

Maybe only a corner.

But a corner matters.

You are not trying to replace the thought with a cheerful one.

You are not trying to say, I am amazing. I am loved. Everything is beautiful.

Those words may be too far away.

They may even feel insulting when the dark is thick.

So we do not start there.

We start with distance.

That is the voice.

This means the thought is something happening in you, not the whole of you.

I do not have to answer it yet.

This means you are allowed to delay belief.

Delay is powerful.

Depression wants immediate agreement.

It wants you to sign the verdict while you are exhausted, hungry, ashamed, alone, and half under the blanket.

The Voice Gap says:

Not yet.

Not never.

Not a big heroic no.

Just not yet.

That tiny delay can be the place where a different next inch becomes possible.

How the Voice Uses Evidence

One reason the voice is hard to resist is that it often brings evidence.

It does not invent everything.

It points to real things and then lies about what they mean.

This is why people in the dark can feel so trapped by it.

If the voice said something obviously false, you might dismiss it.

But it says, Look at the sink.

And the sink is full.

It says, Look at your phone.

And the message is still unanswered.

It says, Look at your hair.

And you know how long it has been since you washed it.

It says, Look at the life you were supposed to have by now.

And there is grief there.

There may be real grief there.

The Voice Gap does not ask you to pretend the evidence is not real.

It asks you to question the sentence the voice builds from it.

A full sink is not a moral diagnosis.

An unanswered message is not proof that you are unlovable.

Unwashed hair is not a character statement.

A life that hurts is not proof that you are the problem.

The voice takes facts and turns them into identity.

The tool helps you turn them back into facts.

This is not small.

When you are depressed, facts are more survivable than verdicts.

A fact can sometimes be met with one clean signal.

A verdict tries to bury you.

If the fact is, There are dishes in the sink, the next inch might be washing one cup.

If the verdict is, I am disgusting, the next inch disappears under shame.

If the fact is, I have not answered my friend, the next inch might be sending:

I am having a hard time. I have not forgotten you.

If the verdict is, I ruin every friendship, the next inch feels pointless.

This is why we practice the gap.

Not to make life suddenly easy.

To make the next inch visible again.

The Five Small Parts of the Voice Gap

If you have enough steadiness, the fuller version of the Voice Gap has five small parts.

Again, these are not steps you have to perform perfectly.

They are not homework.

They are not proof that you are doing recovery correctly.

They are five small places to put your attention when the voice starts turning pain into a verdict.

The first part is Hear It.

This sounds obvious, but it is not.

A voice that has been speaking for a long time can become background noise. You may not notice it until your whole body is already responding.

Your chest is tight.

Your stomach has dropped.

You are scrolling without seeing anything.

You are frozen in the doorway.

You are under the blanket again.

So the first practice is simply noticing:

A sentence is happening.

Not truth.

Not command.

Not prophecy.

A sentence.

The second part is Name It.

You say:

That is the voice.

If you need softer language, you can say:

That sounds like the dark talking.

Or:

That is the old sentence again.

Use the language that does not make you feel foolish.

The words are less important than the separation.

The third part is Delay It.

You say:

I do not have to answer it yet.

This is the heart of the tool.

The voice wants to be believed immediately.

Delay breaks the spell a little.

You can delay for ten seconds.

You can delay until after you drink water.

You can delay until after you text someone.

You can delay until morning.

You are not required to solve the thought before you are allowed to pause it.

The fourth part is Soften It.

You ask:

What is the fact underneath the punishment?

Maybe the fact is that you are tired.

Maybe the fact is that you forgot something.

Maybe the fact is that your room is messy.

Maybe the fact is that you hurt someone and need to make repair when you have enough steadiness.

Softening does not mean excusing everything.

It means removing the cruelty so the truth can be handled.

Cruelty does not make you more responsible.

It usually makes you more frozen.

The fifth part is Choose the Next Inch.

You ask:

What can I do that answers the fact, not the punishment?

If the fact is thirst, drink water.

If the fact is one message, send one honest sentence.

If the fact is a full sink, wash one spoon or leave the room without calling yourself names.

If the fact is danger, reach for help.

If the fact is exhaustion, rest without signing the verdict that rest makes you worthless.

The next inch should be small enough that it does not become another accusation.

If it becomes too big, make it smaller.

If it is still too big, make it smaller again.

If all you can do is say, The voice, that is still the tool.

A Morning Example

Let us make this ordinary.

Not inspirational.

Ordinary.

You wake up late.

Your phone has three notifications.

Your mouth tastes bad.

The room is dim, but not restful.

The first clear thought is:

You are already failing today.

The thought lands before your feet touch the floor.

Your body believes it immediately. Your chest tightens. Your face gets hot. The day, which has barely started, already feels ruined.

The old path would be agreement.

Yes. I am failing. I always fail. What is the point?

The Voice Gap does not require you to leap into confidence.

It only asks for one small interruption.

That is the voice. I do not have to answer it yet.

Then, if you have enough room, you soften it.

What is the fact?

The fact is:

I woke up late.

That is different from:

I am failing today.

The fact may still matter.

There may be consequences.

There may be something you need to adjust.

But the fact is smaller than the verdict.

A smaller thing can be handled more gently.

So you choose the next inch.

Maybe you sit up.

Maybe you put both feet on the floor.

Maybe you drink the water beside the bed.

Maybe you send one message that says:

I am moving slowly today. I will respond when I can.

Maybe the next inch is not even action.

Maybe it is refusing to let the first sentence become the whole day.

That counts.

When the Voice Pretends to Protect You

Sometimes the voice sounds cruel.

Other times, it pretends to protect you.

It says:

Do not answer the message. You will disappoint them anyway.

It says:

Do not try to shower. If you cannot finish, you will feel worse.

It says:

Do not go outside. The light will hurt and then you will crash.

It says:

Do not let anyone see you like this. They will know.

This kind of voice is harder to name because it sounds like caution.

And sometimes caution is valid.

There are days when you do need less light.

There are days when you cannot answer everyone.

There are days when the outside world is too sharp.

The problem is not protection.

The problem is when depression uses protection as a locked door.

A protective voice leaves you with options.

The depressive voice leaves you with a cell.

Protection says, The light is too much right now. Let us dim the room and try again later.

The voice says, You cannot handle the world. Stay hidden.

Protection says, Answer one person when you have enough energy.

The voice says, Do not answer anyone. They are better off without you.

Protection says, Rest. You are tired.

The voice says, Rest because trying is pointless.

The Voice Gap helps you ask a gentle question:

Is this protecting me, or is it shrinking my life without mercy?

You may not know the answer right away.

That is okay.

The question itself creates a little space.

And space is the beginning of the gap.

When You Believe the Voice Anyway

You will believe it sometimes.

Let us say that clearly now.

You will forget the tool.

You will agree with the verdict before you remember there was supposed to be a gap.

You will spend an afternoon inside a sentence that is not kind to you.

You may not realize until night that the dark has been narrating the whole day.

This does not mean you failed.

It means the voice is practiced.

It has had time.

It knows where to press.

A tool you are just learning will not always interrupt a voice that has been rehearsing for years.

So we make room for late practice.

Late still counts.

At the end of the day, when you notice what happened, you can say:

I believed the voice today.

Then add:

That does not mean it was telling the truth.

This is a late Voice Gap.

It may not change the day you just lived.

But it can keep the day from becoming evidence against you forever.

Depression wants to use even your missed practice as proof.

It says, See? You cannot even use the tool.

The gap says:

That is the voice too.

That sentence can become a doorway.

Even if it opens only a crack.

Giving the Voice a Chair, Not the Whole Room

You do not have to pretend the voice is not there.

Sometimes trying to silence it completely makes it louder.

Sometimes arguing with it all day becomes exhausting.

Sometimes the kindest image is not throwing the voice out of the room, but taking away its authority over every chair.

Imagine a small room inside you.

The voice has been sitting in the largest chair, facing the door, making all the decisions.

It has been deciding what every feeling means.

It has been deciding whether you are allowed to rest.

It has been deciding whether a text message proves you are loved or abandoned.

It has been deciding whether a difficult morning means the whole life is ruined.

The Voice Gap does not always remove the voice from the room.

It simply says:

You can sit there, but you do not get the only chair.

There can be another chair for tenderness.

Another for the body.

Another for the part of you that does not know what to believe but still wants to stay.

Another for one person who loves you.

Another for one fact without punishment.

Another for the small tool in your hand.

This is not a fantasy.

It is a way of understanding authority.

The voice may still be present.

But presence is not the same as authority.

A thought can be loud without being in charge.

A sentence can be painful without being final.

A lie can sound like you and still not deserve the whole room.

The One-Minute Practice

If you want a simple practice, use one minute.

Not thirty.

Not a full journaling session.

One minute.

When the voice speaks, pause if you can and ask three questions.

What did the voice say?

What is the fact underneath it?

What is one next inch that answers the fact, not the punishment?

That is the whole practice.

If the voice says, No one cares about you, the fact may be, I feel alone right now.

The next inch may be texting one safe person:

Can you remind me you are there?

If the voice says, You are disgusting, the fact may be, I have not showered.

The next inch may be washing your face, changing your shirt, or deciding that a shower can wait without using the delay as a weapon.

If the voice says, You never finish anything, the fact may be, I did not finish this task.

The next inch may be writing down the first small piece, or choosing rest because the body is done for now.

The practice is not designed to make you impressive.

It is designed to make the sentence smaller.

Smaller sentences are easier to survive.

The Voice Gap and Other People

Other people may not understand this tool at first.

They may hear you say, The voice is loud today, and think you mean an actual sound.

They may try to reassure you too quickly.

They may say, Do not think that way.

They may say, But you know that is not true.

They may mean well.

But the dark is not usually softened by being corrected too fast.

If you have a safe person, you can teach them one sentence.

Please do not argue with the voice first. Help me create a gap.

That might mean they say:

I hear that the voice is saying you are a burden. I am not going to agree with it. Can we wait ten minutes before you believe it?

Or:

Let us answer the fact, not the punishment. Have you eaten today?

Or:

I am here. You do not have to solve the thought while you are this tired.

This can become part of your support language.

Not everyone will know how to use it.

That is okay.

One safe person is enough to begin.

And if there is no safe person available in that moment, you can still say the core sentence to yourself.

That is the voice. I do not have to answer it yet.

You are allowed to be your own small witness until another witness can arrive.

When the Voice Gets Quieter

Sometimes the tool will work in a way you can feel.

The voice will not disappear, but it may move back an inch.

The sentence may lose a little authority.

The room may feel slightly less sealed.

Do not turn that into pressure.

Do not say, Good. Now I should be able to do this every time.

That is the voice borrowing success and turning it into a demand.

A quieter moment is not a contract.

It is only a quieter moment.

Let it be that.

Let the tool help without forcing it to become proof that you are cured.

Book 2 will keep returning to this truth because the dark often turns even progress into pressure. A good day becomes a threat. A completed shower becomes an expectation. One answered message becomes evidence that you should now be available to everyone.

No.

A tool working once means the tool worked once.

That is enough.

The Voice Gap may work today and feel impossible tomorrow.

That does not erase today.

It also does not condemn tomorrow.

We are building a bridge out of small boards, not pouring a highway overnight.

What This Tool Is Really For

The Voice Gap is not here to make you think happy thoughts.

It is not here to help you win debates against depression.

It is not here to shame you for believing the dark.

It is here to give you a little space.

A little space between the sentence and the self.

A little space between the fact and the punishment.

A little space between pain and prophecy.

A little space between the voice and your next inch.

That space may be tiny.

It may last only long enough for you to drink water.

It may last only long enough for you to text, I am not safe alone.

It may last only long enough for you to whisper, Not yet.

But tiny spaces matter in the dark.

A crack under the door is not daylight.

But it is still light.

The voice does not have to vanish for you to survive this moment.

It does not have to become quiet before you are allowed to reach for help.

It does not have to stop speaking before you can choose one clean signal, one breath, one step back, one small act of staying.

You only need enough gap to avoid handing it the whole room.

For today, that may be the bridge.

For Today

When the voice speaks in final sentences, you do not have to believe it immediately.

You can say:

That is the voice. I do not have to answer it yet.

Then choose one next inch that answers the fact, not the punishment.

The voice.

Not truth.

Not command.

Not prophecy.

A sentence.

That may be enough for today.

Chapter 3: One Clean Signal

When the Big Picture Is Too Big

There are days when the big picture is not helpful.

There are days when thinking about your whole life is too much.

Your healing.

Your relationships.

Your body.

Your work.

Your faith.

Your house.

Your future.

Your bills.

Your unread messages.

Your old self.

Your possible self.

All of it can rise at once and stand over you like a mountain.

And when you are already tired, a mountain does not inspire you.

It crushes you.

This is why people can say perfectly reasonable things and still make you feel worse.

You should get back into a routine.

You need to start taking care of yourself.

Maybe if you got up and moved around, you would feel better.

They may be trying to help.

They may even be naming things that matter.

But when the dark is heavy, the big picture turns every suggestion into a threat. A routine sounds like a life you cannot lift. Taking care of yourself sounds like a full-time job. Moving around sounds like proof that if you do not feel better afterward, you failed again.

So we are not going to start with the big picture.

We are going to start with one clean signal.

Not a reset button.

Not a fresh start.

Not a promise that the day will turn around.

One clean signal is one small piece of evidence sent through the dark.

That is all.

The core sentence for this tool is simple:

I do not have to fix the day. I can send one clean signal through it.

If that is too many words, the smallest version is even smaller:

One signal.

That is enough to hold.

That is enough to begin.

Returning to the Shower

Book 1 gave us the shower because the shower is ordinary to people who are not in the dark and enormous to people who are.

To someone outside the room, a shower may look like ten minutes.

To you, it may look like a staircase with too many steps.

Throw off the blanket.

Sit up.

Stand.

Walk.

Turn on the water.

Take off your clothes.

Step in.

Wash your hair.

Wash your body.

Rinse.

Turn off the water.

Step out.

Dry off.

Find something clean enough to wear.

Return to the room changed, but not necessarily better.

That is not nothing.

That is not small in the way the world may call small.

When your body feels like concrete and your mind is moving through fog, a shower can feel like a triathlon. It can require more courage than anyone sees. It can require negotiation with gravity, shame, cold air, hot water, memory, mirror, and exhaustion.

So if anyone has ever made you feel ridiculous for finding the shower hard, let this book say it plainly:

It makes sense that it is hard.

And because it is hard, it can also become a clean signal.

Not because it cures you.

Not because it proves you are fine.

Because it creates one undeniable fact.

You were unwashed.

Now you are washed.

The soap lathered.

The water touched your skin.

The towel dried you.

Something happened in the physical world that the voice cannot easily erase.

Depression may still say, You did nothing today.

But somewhere underneath that sentence, there is another fact:

I washed my body with soap.

It may not feel victorious.

It may not feel meaningful.

You may cry the whole time.

You may hate every second.

The signal still counts.

The soap does not need your optimism.

The water does not need your confidence.

A clean signal is allowed to work mechanically.

Sometimes mechanical is mercy.

What Makes a Signal Clean

A clean signal has three qualities.

It is small enough to finish.

It changes one physical reality.

It closes.

That last part matters more than it may seem.

A clean signal is not the beginning of a long chain of obligations. It is not supposed to open a door to ten more doors. It is not supposed to become, Now that I showered, I should clean the bathroom, answer my emails, cook a real meal, go outside, call everyone back, and become a functioning person by sunset.

No.

That turns the signal into a trap.

A clean signal must be allowed to end.

It needs a period.

Not a comma.

If the signal is a shower, the closed loop might be:

I will wash my body with soap. I will put on clean clothes. Then I am allowed to rest.

If the signal is a cup, the closed loop might be:

I will wash one cup. Then I am done.

If the signal is food, the closed loop might be:

I will eat one thing my body can use. Then I am done.

If the signal is connection, the closed loop might be:

I will send one honest sentence. Then I do not have to manage the whole conversation.

A clean signal is not a productivity system.

It is a mercy system.

It exists because the depressed brain can turn even help into pressure. So we make the action small enough to survive, clear enough to recognize, and closed enough that you do not feel tricked.

This is the agreement:

One signal.

Then rest is still allowed.

If you remove the permission to rest, the tool becomes another demand.

And this book is not here to become another demand.

The Difference Between a Signal and a Task

A task says, Do this because it needs to be done.

A signal says, Do this because it tells the dark something true.

That difference matters.

There are hundreds of tasks around you on any given day. The sink may need attention. The floor may need sweeping. Your body may need food. Your phone may need answers. Your paperwork may need sorting. Your life may be full of things that genuinely need care.

But when everything becomes a task, everything becomes evidence against you.

The laundry is not just laundry.

It becomes proof that you are behind.

The empty glass is not just an empty glass.

It becomes proof that you cannot keep up.

The unopened mail is not just mail.

It becomes proof that your life is unmanageable.

One Clean Signal changes the frame.

It does not ask:

What is everything I should do?

It asks:

What is one small physical fact I can create?

That is gentler.

That is narrower.

That is possible more often than the whole list.

A task may be washing the dishes.

A signal may be washing one spoon.

A task may be cleaning the room.

A signal may be putting all the cups beside the sink.

A task may be making dinner.

A signal may be eating a piece of cheese, a spoonful of peanut butter, soup from a can, toast, or whatever keeps your body from going completely empty.

A task may be reconnecting with everyone.

A signal may be sending one person the truth:

I am having a hard time. I have not forgotten you.

The signal is not less worthy because it is smaller.

It is useful because it is smaller.

It gives you one place to put your hand.

The Signal Families

There are many kinds of clean signals.

The shower is one of them, but it is not the only one.

This matters because some days the shower will be too much. Some days the bathroom will feel too far away. Some days the mirror will be too sharp. Some days your body will not cooperate. Some days the idea of being wet, cold, exposed, or visible to yourself may be more than you can bear.

If the shower is too much, you have not failed the tool.

You choose a smaller signal.

Or a different family.

One Clean Signal has several families: body, room, food, light, sound, connection, and repair.

You do not need all of them.

You only need one.

Body Signals

A body signal tells your body:

You are still here, and I can tend to one small part of you.

It might be washing your face.

It might be brushing your teeth for ten seconds.

It might be changing your shirt.

It might be putting on socks.

It might be wiping your hands with a warm cloth.

It might be drinking water.

It might be taking medication that is already prescribed to you.

It might be sitting up and letting your feet touch the floor.

The body signal does not have to make you feel better.

It only has to create one physical fact.

I drank water.

I changed my shirt.

I touched the floor.

Those facts are not glamorous.

They are not meant to be.

They are small marks in reality.

Room Signals

A room signal changes one inch of the space around you.

Depression can make a room feel like a cave, a nest, a sickroom, a hiding place, and a prison all at once. The air gets heavy. The sheets carry the smell of too many hours. The cups gather. The floor becomes difficult to look at.

You do not have to clean the room.

Cleaning the room may be too much.

A signal is smaller.

Put one cup by the sink.

Throw away one tissue.

Open the curtain one inch.

Move one piece of laundry from the floor to the basket.

Clear the corner of the bed where your hand rests.

Change one pillowcase if changing the sheets is too much.

You are not trying to create a beautiful space.

You are trying to send one message through the static:

This place can change by one inch.

One inch is not the whole room.

But one inch is not nothing.

Food Signals

A food signal answers the body before it becomes another judge.

Depression can disrupt hunger in both directions. You may not feel hungry at all. You may feel hollow and still unable to choose food. You may eat whatever is easiest and then let the voice punish you for it.

We are not going to turn food into another moral test.

A clean food signal is not about eating perfectly.

It is about giving the body one usable thing.

A glass of water.

A banana.

A boiled egg.

A piece of toast.

A handful of nuts.

A cup of soup.

A protein drink.

A leftover bite of something from the fridge.

If all you can manage is something simple, simple counts.

If all you can manage is something imperfect, imperfect counts.

The signal is not:

I ate correctly.

The signal is:

I gave my body something.

That is enough for this tool.

Light Signals

A light signal changes your relationship to the room without forcing you into brightness.

This is important in this series because we already know that light can hurt.

We are not going to throw open every curtain and call that healing.

A light signal may be very small.

Turn on one lamp instead of the overhead light.

Open the curtain only a finger-width.

Sit near a window without looking outside.

Step onto the porch for one breath.

Let morning light touch the wall, not your face.

Dim the room if the light is too sharp.

Yes, dimming the room can be a clean signal too.

A clean signal is not always more light.

Sometimes it is wiser light.

Sometimes it is choosing the amount of light your body can survive today.

The signal says:

I can adjust the world by one small degree.

Sound Signals

A sound signal interrupts the silence or softens the noise.

The dark can make silence feel thick.

It can also make sound feel unbearable.

So again, we do not force one answer.

A sound signal might be turning on a familiar song at low volume.

It might be playing rain sounds.

It might be turning off the television that has been shouting in the background.

It might be putting in earplugs.

It might be stepping away from a room where voices are too much.

It might be listening to one voice note from someone safe.

The signal is not:

I created the perfect atmosphere.

The signal is:

I changed what is reaching me.

That can matter.

Especially when your nervous system feels scraped raw.

Connection Signals

A connection signal reaches toward another human without asking you to manage the whole relationship.

This one needs care.

Connection can help.

Connection can also feel like pressure.

So we keep it closed.

One sentence.

One person.

No requirement to perform wellness.

You might write:

I am having a hard day. No need to fix it. Just wanted to say I am here.

Or:

Can you send me one ordinary thing from your day? I need a small tether.

Or:

I do not have energy to talk, but I wanted you to know I am alive and trying.

Or, if safety is involved:

I should not be alone right now. Can you stay with me or help me reach someone who can?

If you are in immediate danger, reach emergency support. If you are in the United States and might hurt yourself, call or text 988.

The clean signal in that moment is not a small chore.

It is reaching for rescue.

A connection signal is not a conversation contract.

It is a flare.

A small one.

Enough to say:

I am still here.

Repair Signals

A repair signal is for the place where depression has left a tear.

This one is optional.

Use it carefully.

Repair can become shame very quickly.

You may look at all the things you have not answered, all the plans you canceled, all the ways you have withdrawn, and feel crushed by the need to make everything right.

Do not make repair into a mountain.

A repair signal is one stitch.

Not the whole seam.

You might say:

I am sorry I went quiet. I have been in a hard place. I care about you.

Or:

I cannot explain everything right now, but I wanted to reconnect with one honest sentence.

Or:

I missed this, and I am sorry. I am not able to fix it all today, but I wanted to acknowledge it.

That is a clean signal.

It does not repair every consequence.

It does not erase pain.

It does not demand that the other person respond perfectly.

It only creates one honest fact where silence had been growing.

One stitch is not the whole seam.

But it is a stitch.

How to Choose Your Signal

When everything feels impossible, choosing can become its own burden.

So do not ask:

What would fix the most?

Ask:

What is the smallest closed loop I can complete without lying to myself?

That question is kinder.

It respects the actual amount of energy in the room.

You can choose by location.

If you are in bed, the signal might be drinking water, sitting up, changing your shirt, or putting one cup on the floor beside the door so it can leave the room later.

You can choose by pain.

If your mouth feels stale, brush for ten seconds.

If your skin feels wrong, wash your hands or face.

If the silence feels thick, turn on one soft sound.

If the light feels cruel, adjust the curtain.

You can choose by shame.

If one particular thing is becoming a verdict, make the smallest possible move near it.

Not the whole thing.

Near it.

If the voice keeps pointing at the sink, wash one cup.

If it keeps pointing at the phone, send one sentence.

If it keeps pointing at the bed, straighten one corner or change one pillowcase.

You are not obeying shame.

You are shrinking the battlefield.

And if even choosing is too much, use the smallest version:

One signal.

Then do the first small thing your hand can reach.

Drink the water.

Move the cup.

Open the wrapper.

Touch the floor.

That counts.

Permission to Stop

This is the part we have to protect.

After one clean signal, you are allowed to stop.

You are allowed to go back to bed.

You are allowed to return to the couch.

You are allowed to sit in the quiet.

You are allowed to rest without turning rest into an insult.

This permission is not laziness.

It is how the tool stays usable.

If your brain learns that one signal always leads to ten demands, it will resist the signal. It will know the trap before you begin. It will say, Do not start, because starting means you will be forced to keep going.

So we tell the truth from the beginning.

One signal means one signal.

If more comes, fine.

If no more comes, the signal still counts.

You may shower and then go directly back to bed.

You may wash one cup and leave the rest.

You may eat one thing and not make a meal.

You may send one message and not answer the reply right away.

You may open the curtain and close it again if the light is too much.

The signal does not become invalid because you rested afterward.

The rest may be the reason the signal was possible.

When the Signal Does Not Change Your Mood

A clean signal may not make you feel better.

This is not a failure.

It is important to say that plainly because many people give up on small tools when they do not create an immediate emotional shift.

You may wash your face and still feel empty.

You may eat and still feel numb.

You may send the message and still feel alone.

You may shower and still want the dark room afterward.

The signal did not fail just because your mood did not transform.

The purpose of the signal is not always to change how you feel.

Sometimes the purpose is to create a fact that can stand beside the feeling.

The feeling says, Nothing can move.

The fact says, One thing moved.

The feeling says, I am completely lost.

The fact says, I drank water.

The feeling says, I am disappearing.

The fact says, I sent one sentence to someone safe.

Facts do not always comfort you immediately.

But they can become small stones under your feet.

Not enough for the whole bridge.

Enough for the next step.

Late Practice Still Counts

You may remember this tool after the moment has passed.

You may spend the whole day under the verdict, then realize at night that one signal might have helped.

That still counts.

Late practice is still practice.

You can look back without using the looking back as a weapon.

You can say:

Today I did not send a clean signal when the dark got loud.

Then you can add:

That does not mean I failed. It means I can choose one now, or try again tomorrow.

Maybe the late signal is putting water beside the bed.

Maybe it is taking medication before sleep if that belongs to your care.

Maybe it is plugging in your phone.

Maybe it is placing a clean shirt where morning can find it.

Maybe it is writing one note:

One signal tomorrow. Not the whole day.

Late does not erase the tool.

Late can prepare the ground.

Depression will try to turn missed practice into another verdict.

It will say, You could not even do one small thing.

The Voice Gap from the last chapter can answer:

That is the voice. I do not have to answer it yet.

Then One Clean Signal can add:

I can send one signal now.

The tools can hold hands.

They are allowed to work together.

If Someone Wants to Help

If someone in your life wants to help, this is a tool they can understand.

Not by commanding it.

Not by saying, Go take a shower.

Not by turning one clean signal into a test of your willingness to get better.

They can help by lowering the cost of the signal.

They can bring water to the bed.

They can place a clean towel in the bathroom.

They can change the sheets while you shower.

They can sit outside the bathroom door if being alone feels too hard.

They can wash the cup and leave it where you can reach it.

They can send one text that does not require a performance:

No need to reply. I am here.

They can ask:

Would it help if I made the first step smaller?

That is often better than advice.

Advice points at the mountain.

Support removes one stone.

If you are the one receiving help, you are allowed to be specific.

You can say:

Please do not tell me everything I need to do. Can you help me do one clean signal?

Or:

Can you bring me water and not ask questions right now?

Or:

Can you remind me I am allowed to rest after this?

That last one matters.

Sometimes what you need most is not motivation.

It is permission not to be trapped by the next thing.

What One Clean Signal Is Really For

One Clean Signal is not here to turn you into a productive person.

It is not here to impress anyone.

It is not here to prove you are healed.

It is not here to build a perfect morning routine.

It is here to interrupt the static.

It is here to create one fact where depression has been creating verdicts.

It is here to remind your body that one small change can still happen.

It is here to give your hands something honest to do when your mind is too full of fog to reason with.

Some days, that one fact will be a shower.

Some days, it will be a cup of water.

Some days, it will be one text.

Some days, it will be opening the curtain a finger-width.

Some days, it will be calling for help because the dark has become too dangerous to sit with alone.

All of those can be clean signals if they answer the actual moment without turning into a punishment.

You do not have to fix the day.

You do not have to fix the week.

You do not have to become the version of yourself other people keep waiting for.

You only have to ask:

What is one small piece of evidence I can send through the dark?

Then let it be enough for now.

Not forever.

For now.

For today.

For Today

You do not have to build momentum today.

You do not have to turn one action into a whole life.

Choose one clean signal.

Make it small.

Make it closed.

Then let yourself rest without taking the signal away from yourself.

One signal.

That may be enough for today.

Chapter 4: Breath and Step Back

When the Feeling Becomes the Whole Room

Sometimes the dark does not arrive slowly.

Sometimes it floods.

One moment you are standing in the kitchen, answering a question, reading a message, looking at the light through the window, or trying to make one small decision.

Then something shifts.

Your chest tightens.

Your breath gets shallow.

The room feels louder than it was a minute ago.

The light feels sharper.

The thoughts begin arriving too quickly to sort.

One thought becomes ten.

Ten becomes a courtroom.

The courtroom becomes a storm.

And suddenly you are not just having a feeling.

You are inside it.

It fills the room. It fills your body. It fills the space between what happened and what you believe it means. It takes one moment and tries to make it your whole life.

This is when people may tell you to calm down.

But calm down is not a tool.

Calm down is often just a command someone gives when your pain has become inconvenient or frightening to them. It can make you feel ashamed for having a nervous system that is already overwhelmed. It can make you feel like you are failing again because your body did not obey on cue.

So we are not going to begin with calm.

We are going to begin with space.

The core sentence for this tool is:

I can breathe once and step back before I become the whole feeling.

If that is too many words, the smallest version is:

One breath.

That is where we start.

Not peace.

Not clarity.

Not a perfect response.

One breath.

One inch of space.

One chance to remember that the feeling is real, but it is not the whole of you.

The Body Under Alarm

Book 1 named the body honestly.

The concrete in the legs.

The vacuum in the chest.

The gravity in the room.

The marionette feeling, where you are somewhere far away, trying to operate your own arms and voice with strings that keep slipping from your hands.

The strange body.

The body that feels too heavy, too hollow, too raw, too numb, or too loud to inhabit comfortably.

If you recognized those descriptions, then you already know something important.

Depression is not only a thought problem.

It lives in the body.

It changes the way air feels. It changes the way sound lands. It changes the distance between the bed and the door. It changes the weight of an unanswered text. It changes the way your own name sounds when someone says it from another room.

When the body is under alarm, it may not ask your permission before reacting.

Your shoulders may rise.

Your jaw may lock.

Your stomach may turn.

Your hands may go cold.

Your heart may pound or sink.

Your breath may climb into the top of your chest and stay there.

You may feel like you need to escape, hide, explain, apologize, disappear, defend yourself, or shut down completely.

None of this means you are dramatic.

None of this means you are weak.

It means your body is trying to protect you from something it has registered as too much.

Maybe the threat is real.

Maybe the threat is memory.

Maybe the threat is a tone of voice, a crowded room, a familiar silence, a kind message you do not know how to answer, or a splinter of light that hurts because it reminds you of what you miss.

The body does not always know the difference.

It only knows that the alarm has started.

Breath and Step Back is not here to shame the alarm.

It is here to give you one small handle when the alarm gets loud.

The Goal Is Not to Calm Down

This needs to be said clearly.

The first goal of Breath and Step Back is not to calm down.

Calm may come.

It may not.

The feeling may soften.

It may stay.

The tightness in your chest may loosen a little, or it may remain exactly where it is. The thought may still be loud. The room may still feel too bright. Your hands may still shake. Your body may still want to run, freeze, or fold inward.

That does not mean the tool failed.

The goal is smaller than calm.

The goal is one inch of space.

Space between the feeling and the story.

Space between the alarm and the action.

Space between the thought and the verdict.

Space between the splinter and the wound it touches.

When there is no space, the feeling becomes everything.

A message is not just a message.

It becomes proof that everyone is tired of you.

A hard morning is not just a hard morning.

It becomes proof that nothing will ever change.

A body sensation is not just a body sensation.

It becomes proof that you cannot survive the day.

A small mistake is not just a small mistake.

It becomes a sentence handed down by the courtroom.

Breath and Step Back interrupts that collapse.

It does not argue with the feeling.

It does not dismiss it.

It does not tell you to be grateful, positive, rational, spiritual, cheerful, or strong.

It only creates enough space to say:

Something is happening in me. I do not have to become it immediately.

That is the emergency brake.

Not a cure.

A brake.

The Four-Part Practice

The full version of Breath and Step Back has four parts.

Breathe once.

Step back.

Name what is happening.

Choose one tiny response.

That is it.

If four parts feel like too many, return to the smallest version:

One breath.

The smallest version still counts.

Breathe Once

Do not begin with a breathing routine.

Begin with one breath.

Not a perfect breath.

Not a beautiful breath.

Not a breath that proves you are centered and wise and handling everything gracefully.

Just one honest breath.

You may not be able to take a deep breath.

That is okay.

Sometimes the vacuum in the chest makes a deep breath feel impossible. Sometimes asking for a deep breath only makes you more aware that your body feels locked.

So do not force depth.

Let the breath be the size it is.

You can inhale a little.

You can exhale a little longer if you can.

You can place a hand on your chest, your stomach, the chair, the blanket, the counter, or the wall.

You can say quietly:

One breath.

The breath is not there to fix the feeling.

It is there to mark a pause.

It is a small line in the sand between the flood and your next move.

Step Back

Stepping back may be physical.

It may also be internal.

If you are standing too close to the sink, the doorway, the phone, the mirror, the argument, or the task, you may take one actual step back.

One step away from the counter.

One step away from the screen.

One step into the hall.

One step to sit down.

One step out of the room if it is safe and appropriate to leave.

But sometimes your body cannot move.

Sometimes stepping back means softening your grip on the phone.

Looking at the floor instead of the message.

Turning your face away from the harsh light.

Unclenching your jaw by one degree.

Letting your shoulders drop a fraction.

Imagining yourself taking one step back from the feeling, even if your feet stay exactly where they are.

The point is not distance.

The point is separation.

You are giving yourself a little space to notice the feeling instead of being swallowed by it.

Name What Is Happening

Naming is not explaining.

You do not need to understand the whole history of the feeling.

You do not need to know why this moment hit so hard.

You do not need to write a report for anyone.

You only need a plain name.

This is overwhelm.

This is shame.

This is fear.

This is the voice getting loud.

This is my body under alarm.

This is a splinter.

This is too much sound.

This is too much light.

This is the old courtroom starting again.

The name does not have to be perfect.

It only has to be honest enough to create a little distance.

When you name what is happening, you are no longer only inside it.

You are also observing it.

That observation is small.

But small is what we are practicing.

Choose One Tiny Response

After you breathe once, step back, and name what is happening, choose one tiny response.

Not the best response.

Not the most impressive response.

Not the response that repairs your whole life.

One tiny response.

If the light is too much, soften the light.

If the sound is too much, lower the sound or leave the room.

If the message is too much, put the phone face down and decide when to return to it.

If the voice is loud, use the Voice Gap:

That is the voice. I do not have to answer it yet.

If the day feels impossible, send One Clean Signal:

One signal. Then rest is still allowed.

If the feeling is dangerous and you might hurt yourself, the tiny response is not to sit alone and practice harder.

The response is to reach for help immediately.

If you are in the United States, call or text 988. If there is immediate danger, contact emergency services or go to the nearest emergency room. You do not have to survive a dangerous moment by being privately brave.

A tiny response can be rescue.

A tiny response can be leaving the room.

A tiny response can be drinking water.

A tiny response can be saying:

I need a minute.

A tiny response can be doing nothing for ten seconds instead of saying the cruel thing to yourself.

The point is not to choose perfectly.

The point is to choose with one inch more space than you had before.

When the Feeling Does Not Leave

You may breathe once and still feel terrible.

You may step back and still feel flooded.

You may name the feeling and still believe it.

You may choose one tiny response and still want to disappear into the dark.

That does not mean you did it wrong.

This tool is not a magic door.

It is a hinge.

A hinge does not move the whole house.

It only gives one part of the house the ability to open a little.

Sometimes that little opening is enough to keep you from doing harm.

Sometimes it is enough to keep you from sending the message you would regret.

Sometimes it is enough to help you sit down before your body collapses.

Sometimes it is enough to let you say, I am overwhelmed, instead of I am broken.

And sometimes it will feel like nothing changed at all.

Even then, the practice counts.

One breath counts even if the feeling stays.

One step back counts even if the room is still loud.

One name counts even if the name trembles.

One tiny response counts even if you have to rest afterward.

Late practice still counts here too.

If you only remember this tool after the storm has already passed, you can still practice gently.

You can look back and say:

That was overwhelm.

My body was under alarm.

Next time, I can try one breath.

That is not failure.

That is learning the shape of your own weather.

A Simple Example

Imagine you receive a message that says:

Can we talk later?

That is all it says.

No anger.

No explanation.

No threat.

But your body does not read it as neutral.

Your chest tightens.

Your stomach drops.

Your mind starts building the case.

They are mad.

You did something wrong.

They are leaving.

You are too much.

You should fix this immediately.

You should apologize before you even know what happened.

This is where Breath and Step Back begins.

One breath.

Maybe it is shallow.

Maybe it barely reaches your ribs.

It still counts.

Step back.

Put the phone on the table.

Turn it face down.

Let your eyes look at something else in the room.

Name what is happening.

This is fear.

Or:

This is the old courtroom.

Or:

This is my body treating uncertainty like danger.

Then choose one tiny response.

Maybe the response is waiting ten minutes before replying.

Maybe it is sending one steady sentence:

Yes. I am feeling anxious, but I can talk later.

Maybe it is asking for context:

Yes. Is everything okay, or should I prepare for something serious?

Maybe it is reaching for support before answering because the fear is too loud.

The tool does not guarantee the conversation will be easy.

It only helps you not become the fear before you have more information.

That is enough.

Another Example

Imagine you are in a room where everything is too much.

The television is on.

Someone is talking in the kitchen.

A light is flickering.

Your shirt feels wrong against your skin.

Your thoughts are moving too quickly.

You can feel yourself slipping toward shutdown.

This is not the time to make a full plan.

This is the time for the emergency brake.

One breath.

Step back.

Maybe you move to the doorway.

Maybe you sit on the floor.

Maybe you close your eyes for one second.

Name what is happening.

This is too much sound.

This is too much light.

My body is overloaded.

Choose one tiny response.

Turn off the television if you can.

Ask for the light to be changed.

Step into the bathroom for two minutes.

Put on a softer shirt.

Text someone safe:

I am overloaded. I need quiet.

You are not being difficult.

You are responding to overload.

There is a difference.

If Someone Is With You

If someone you trust is nearby, Breath and Step Back can become a shared language.

Not a command.

A language.

They should not bark, Breathe, at you like you are a problem to control.

They should not use the tool to rush you into calm.

They can say, gently:

Do you need one breath and a step back?

Or:

Do you want me to help make the room smaller?

Or:

Do you want quiet, water, space, or company?

That kind of help gives options without adding pressure.

If you are able, you can tell them what helps before the emergency comes.

You might say:

When I get overwhelmed, please do not ask me many questions. Remind me to breathe once and give me space.

Or:

If I say I need to step back, please let me leave the room without making me explain right away.

Or:

If I seem dangerous to myself, please stay with me and help me reach crisis support.

The people who love you may need simple instructions because fear can make them loud too.

This tool can help both sides remember:

The goal is not pressure.

The goal is space.

How This Tool Connects to the Others

Breath and Step Back does not replace the first three tools.

It gathers them.

The Splinter Pause helps you notice the painful flash of light without turning it into a whole story.

The Voice Gap helps you hear the lie without immediately believing it.

One Clean Signal gives your hands one small physical fact to create.

Breath and Step Back helps you reach any of those tools when the feeling is flooding the room.

It is the space-maker.

It says:

Wait.

One breath.

Step back.

Name it.

Choose small.

You do not have to do this beautifully.

You do not have to remember every step every time.

If all you remember is one breath, that is still part of the tool.

If all you remember is step back, that is still part of the tool.

If all you do is name the feeling after it already swallowed you, that is still practice.

The bridge is not built by perfect moments.

It is built by returning.

Again and again.

With less shame when you can.

With help when you need it.

With rest afterward.

For Today

You do not have to calm the whole storm today.

You do not have to become steady all at once.

Take one breath.

Step back by one inch if you can.

Name what is happening without turning it into a verdict.

Then choose one tiny response, and let that be enough for now.

One breath.

That may be enough for today.

Chapter 5: Building a Safe Room in Your Mind

There are moments when the outside world becomes too loud to belong to.

The room is too bright.

The voices are too sharp.

The phone is too much.

The air itself feels crowded.

And sometimes it is not even the outside world. Sometimes the noise is coming from inside you. Your thoughts are pacing. Your body is sounding alarms. Your chest is tight, your stomach is clenched, your skin feels strange, and your mind keeps opening doors you do not want to walk through.

In Book 1, we talked about how depression can start to feel like the house itself.

Not a visitor in the house.

Not a storm passing over it.

The house.

We talked about how the dark can become familiar. How a closed bedroom door can feel safer than the bright and demanding world outside it. How the dark is not actually keeping you safe, but it can feel like the closest thing to safe when everything else asks too much of you.

That truth still matters.

I am not going to take it away from you.

There are reasons you learned to retreat. There are reasons you learned to close the door. There are reasons your body may reach for darkness, quiet, blankets, distance, and stillness when life becomes too much.

You were not being dramatic.

You were trying to survive.

But there is a difference between a room that traps you and a room that shelters you.

There is a difference between hiding because you have disappeared and resting because you are still here.

There is a difference between the dark getting every chair in the house and you keeping one small corner for yourself.

That is what this chapter is about.

Not pretending the dark is gone.

Not forcing yourself into a bright, cheerful place you do not believe in.

Not building an imaginary mansion of perfect peace and then feeling like a failure because your mind will not stay there.

This is smaller than that.

This is gentler than that.

This is the practice of building one safe room inside you.

One small room where the dark does not get every chair.

The Room You Learned to Survive In

When you have lived in the dark for a long time, your inner world can start to feel like one room.

The same walls.

The same stale air.

The same blanket pulled over your head.

The same voice in the corner telling you nothing will change.

The same bed, the same ceiling, the same ache in your body, the same distance between you and the door.

Depression is very good at making one room feel like the whole world.

From inside it, the walls look final. The door looks sealed. The window looks painted shut. The dark says, this is all there is. This is where you live now. This is where you belong.

But the dark lies about size.

It makes itself seem bigger than it is.

It makes one room feel like the earth.

In Book 1, we said that the walls of the room are not the edges of the earth. I want to return to that gently now, because Book 2 is where we begin to place tools under the truths we already named.

If the dark has convinced you it owns the whole house, the safe room practice begins by making one small exception.

Not the whole house.

Not every room.

Not your whole life.

Just one small inner room the dark does not get to arrange completely.

A chair.

A lamp.

A blanket.

A door that closes softly.

A window that does not have to open yet.

One object that belongs to you.

One corner where you can breathe without being cross-examined.

This is not childish.

This is not silly.

This is not pretending.

Your mind already builds rooms. It builds courtrooms where you are accused. It builds prisons where you are punished. It builds dark bedrooms where you disappear. It builds stages where you perform being fine. It builds hallways of memory you did not ask to walk through again.

If your mind can build places that hurt you, it can also learn to build one place that helps you stay.

Not perfectly.

Not all at once.

But enough to give you one small refuge when the rest of the house is loud.

What the Safe Room Is Not

Before we build it, I want to be very clear about what this tool is not.

The safe room is not denial.

It is not a way of saying the pain is not real. It is not a way of painting over grief, fear, shame, trauma, exhaustion, or depression with a pretty picture.

It is not a command to relax.

It is not a test of whether you are spiritual enough, imaginative enough, calm enough, or healed enough.

It is not a place where you must feel peaceful.

That matters.

Some people hear the word safe and immediately feel pressure. They think, if I build a safe room in my mind, I am supposed to feel safe. And if I do not feel safe, then I failed the exercise.

No.

You did not fail.

A safe room is not a guarantee of a feeling.

It is a structure.

It is a place to set the feeling down for one second. It is a room where fear can sit in a chair without driving the whole car. It is a place where shame can be present without being handed the microphone. It is a place where depression can knock on the door without being allowed to rearrange all the furniture.

You may still feel anxious inside the safe room.

You may still feel numb.

You may still feel heavy.

You may still feel like you are making it up.

That does not mean the room is not working.

It means you are practicing while still being human.

The safe room is also not an escape from responsibility or reality. It is not where you go to avoid your whole life forever. It is not a permanent address.

It is a pause.

A shelter.

A small interior place to gather yourself before you return to the next breath, the next room, the next conversation, the next glass of water, the next human hand.

Think of it like stepping into a quiet hallway during a loud gathering.

You have not left the building.

You have not solved everything.

You have simply found a place where your nervous system can stop being touched by every sound at once.

That is enough.

The Tool

The safe room practice has four parts.

First, choose the room.

Second, place a few anchors inside it.

Third, give the room a boundary.

Fourth, return to it in the smallest possible way.

That is all.

You do not need to see it perfectly. You do not need to turn it into a movie in your mind. You do not need a vivid imagination. You do not need to close your eyes if closing your eyes makes you feel worse.

You can build this room with words.

You can build it with one picture.

You can build it with a phrase.

You can build it with a physical gesture.

You can build it with the memory of a room you once loved, or the idea of a room you never had.

It can be real.

It can be imagined.

It can be borrowed from a library, a grandmother's kitchen, a church basement, a cabin, a hospital waiting room where one person was kind to you, a corner of your bedroom, a porch, a garden shed, a car parked under a tree, or a room that exists only because you need it to.

The only rule is that the room must not demand performance from you.

You do not have to smile there.

You do not have to explain there.

You do not have to improve there.

You do not have to be grateful there.

You do not have to become someone easier to love there.

You are allowed to enter as you are.

Tired.

Angry.

Numb.

Ashamed.

Afraid.

Blank.

Uncertain.

Still here.

Choosing the Room

Do not start with beauty.

Start with relief.

Beauty can come later, if it comes at all.

Ask yourself:

What kind of room would ask the least of me?

Not what room would impress someone else.

Not what room looks like healing.

Not what room proves I am doing better.

What room would ask the least of me?

Maybe it is dim, but not dark.

Maybe there is one lamp with a warm shade.

Maybe there is a chair that does not expect you to sit up straight.

Maybe there is a blanket with enough weight to remind your body where it ends.

Maybe there is a door, and the door has a lock, but the lock is not a prison. It is a choice.

Maybe there is a window, but the window does not flood the room with light. It lets in only as much as you can bear.

Maybe there is no window at all.

That is allowed.

Maybe there is a small table with a glass of water already waiting.

Maybe there is a dog asleep on the floor.

Maybe there are books, but no one expects you to read them.

Maybe there is a candle, but it does not have to fix the darkness.

Maybe there is nothing but a mattress on the floor and one clean sheet.

Let the room be plain.

Plain is often safer than perfect.

Perfect rooms can become another kind of pressure. They can start asking you to maintain them, decorate them, explain them, make them worthy.

This room does not need to be worthy.

It only needs to hold you for a moment.

Placing the Anchors

Once you have some sense of the room, give it a few anchors.

An anchor is something your mind can touch when everything inside you is moving too fast.

One chair.

One lamp.

One blanket.

One door.

One window.

One object.

That is plenty.

If your mind wants to add more, let it.

If your mind goes blank, keep only one.

A chair is enough.

A lamp is enough.

A blanket is enough.

A doorknob is enough.

Your anchor does not need to be meaningful.
Sometimes meaningful things are too loaded.
Sometimes they bring memories with them.
Sometimes they open doors you are not ready to open.

A plain object can be merciful.

A blue mug.

A wooden chair.

A folded towel.

A stone on a windowsill.

A quilt with no story attached.

A lamp that simply turns on.

When the mind is flooded, simplicity is kind.

You are not building a museum of your life. You are building a room where you can sit down without being attacked by every memory you have ever carried.

If a chosen object starts to hurt, remove it.

You are allowed to change the room.

You are allowed to take out the photograph.

You are allowed to move the chair.

You are allowed to close the window.

You are allowed to lock the door.

You are allowed to leave the light on.

You are allowed to turn the light off.

The room belongs to your survival, not to an aesthetic.

Giving the Room a Boundary

A safe room needs a boundary.

Not because the world is bad.

Not because people who love you are enemies.

Not because you should disappear.

Because a room without a boundary is not a refuge. It is just another place where everything can rush in.

The boundary can be simple.

A door.

A curtain.

A line of light under the door.

A phrase.

A hand over your heart.

A palm against your thigh.

A small breath before you answer.

You might say:

Only what helps me stay can come in here right now.

You might say:

Not every thought gets a chair.

You might say:

Shame can wait outside.

You might say:

I am not available for the courtroom right now.

You might say nothing at all.

You might simply imagine the door closing softly.

Softly matters.

This is not a slammed door.

This is not rage against yourself.

This is not a war with your thoughts.

This is a boundary that sounds like mercy.

There will be days when the dark still gets in.

Of course there will.

There will be days when the room feels flimsy. Days when the walls look thin. Days when the voice of depression sits in the corner even after you told it to wait outside.

That does not mean you failed.

It means the room is still under construction.

You can build while afraid.

You can build while numb.

You can build while the dark complains.

If You Cannot Visualize

Some people can close their eyes and see a room clearly.

Some people cannot.

Some people see only black.

Some people see fragments.

Some people feel more anxious when they try to imagine anything. Some people have minds that work better in words than pictures. Some people have memories that make interior exercises feel unsafe or unpredictable.

If that is you, you are not excluded from this tool.

You do not have to see the room.

You can name it.

Safe room.

You can choose one word.

Lamp.

Chair.

Blanket.

Door.

You can place your hand against your chest and let that be the room.

You can press your feet into the floor and let the floor be the room.

You can wrap your fingers around a mug, a stone, a sleeve, or the edge of a blanket and let that object be the room.

You can write one phrase on a piece of paper and keep it near your bed.

One small room.

Not every thought gets a chair.

The dark does not get every seat.

I can sit here for one breath.

You can use sound instead of image.

A quiet hum.

A fan.

Rain.

The imagined click of a door closing.

You can use touch instead of image.

Your thumb against your finger.

Your hand on your ribs.

A blanket over your shoulders.

You can use a real place instead of an imagined one.

A corner of the couch.

The bathroom with the light off and the door cracked.

The front seat of your car.

The edge of your bed.

The safe room does not have to live only in imagination. Sometimes your body needs a real object to believe the instruction.

That is not weakness.

That is wisdom.

When the Room Gets Loud Anyway

There will be moments when you try to enter the safe room and your mind follows you in with muddy shoes.

The voice comes in.

The shame comes in.

The memory comes in.

The fear comes in.

The body alarm comes in.

You may think:

This did not work.

But remember what we are practicing in this book.

We are not measuring success by whether the feeling leaves.

We are measuring success by whether you found one inch of space.

In Chapter 1, we practiced The Splinter Pause. Notice one small thing without forcing it to become hope.

In Chapter 2, we practiced The Voice Gap. Hear the thought without immediately bowing to it.

In Chapter 3, we practiced One Clean Signal. Send one small message to your body or environment that says, I am still here.

In Chapter 4, we practiced Breath and Step Back. Breathe once before you become the whole feeling.

The safe room gathers those tools into one place.

You might enter the room and notice one splinter of light, even if it hurts.

You might hear the voice say, this is stupid, and leave a gap before believing it.

You might send one clean signal by pulling a blanket around your shoulders.

You might breathe once and step back from the flood.

That is the room working.

Not because it made you peaceful.

Because it gave you somewhere to place your feet.

Late practice still counts.

If you only remember the safe room after the spiral has already started, that still counts.

If you only think the word chair while crying, that still counts.

If you only put your hand on your chest and whisper safe room without feeling safe, that still counts.

If you forget the tool completely and remember it tomorrow, that still counts too.

We are building a path by walking it badly, then walking it again.

When You Are Not Safe

I want to place a clear handrail here.

A safe room in your mind can be a refuge, but it is not a substitute for safety in the real world.

If you are in immediate danger, if someone else is hurting you, if you might hurt yourself, or if you do not trust yourself to stay alive, the safe room is not enough by itself.

The next right step is not to practice harder alone.

The next right step is to reach another human being.

If you are in the United States, you can call or text 988 for the Suicide and Crisis Lifeline. If there is immediate danger, contact emergency services or go to the nearest emergency room.

The safe room can help you take the breath before you reach out.

It can help you find the sentence.

It can help you stay for the next minute.

But it should not become a locked door between you and help.

That is not what this tool is for.

This tool is a shelter.

It is not a bunker where you must suffer silently.

If the dark is asking you to be alone with danger, that is not safety. That is the dark trying to isolate you.

Let another human being into the hallway.

You do not have to explain perfectly.

You can say:

I am not safe by myself.

You can say:

I need help staying here.

You can say:

Please sit with me.

That sentence is allowed to be the door.

The Smallest Version

The smallest version of this tool is not the full room.

It is not the chair, the lamp, the blanket, the door, the window, the object, the boundary, and the breath.

The smallest version is two words.

Safe room.

That is all.

When your mind is crowded, you can say:

Safe room.

When shame starts rearranging the furniture, you can say:

Safe room.

When the phone buzzes and your body locks up, you can say:

Safe room.

When the house is loud and you cannot find yourself inside it, you can say:

Safe room.

When you are lying in bed and the ceiling feels too far away, you can say:

Safe room.

You may not feel safe.

Say it anyway.

Not as a lie.

As a direction.

Safe room does not mean I am safe right now in every way.

It means I am turning toward shelter.

It means I am looking for the chair the dark does not get.

It means I am giving myself one small corner that does not belong entirely to the pain.

That is enough for today.

The Chair the Dark Does Not Get

I keep coming back to the chair because it is simple.

A chair does not fix the house.

A chair does not repair the roof.

A chair does not make the weather change.

A chair does not ask you to believe in a bright future before you are ready.

A chair only says:

Sit here for a moment.

Rest your body.

Stop standing trial.

Stop performing.

Stop explaining.

Let the room hold you without asking you to become impressive.

Maybe that is all the safe room is at first.

A chair the dark does not get.

One place inside you where you do not have to argue for your right to exist.

One lamp that does not interrogate you.

One blanket that does not accuse you of hiding.

One door that closes softly, not to keep help out, but to keep shame from running the room.

One window that lets in only the amount of light you can bear.

You do not have to move into this room forever.

You do not have to decorate it perfectly.

You do not have to invite anyone in before you are ready.

You only have to know it is there.

And if you cannot know it yet, you can borrow my knowing for a while.

There can be one small room inside you where the dark does not get every chair.

There can be one place where the voice is not in charge.

There can be one corner where your body is allowed to be tired without being hated.

There can be one breath that belongs to you.

Not the whole house.

Not the whole life.

Not the whole future.

One room.

One chair.

One breath.

Safe room.

For Today

You do not have to feel safe everywhere.

You do not have to open every window.

You do not have to leave the dark all at once.

For today, try building one small room inside you where the dark does not get every chair.

It can be nothing more than a word.

Safe room.

It can be nothing more than your hand on your chest.

It can be nothing more than imagining one chair, one lamp, one blanket, or one softly closed door.

If the room does not feel safe yet, you have not failed.

You are learning the shape of shelter.

And if you are unsafe, please do not stay alone inside the room. Reach for another human being. Call or text 988 if you are in the United States. Contact emergency services if there is immediate danger.

The safe room is not where you disappear.

It is where you remember you are still here.

I can build one small room inside me where the dark does not get every chair.

Safe room.

That may be enough for today.

Chapter 6: Navigating the Good Days

When the Light Feels Like a Question

There is a strange fear that can arrive on a better morning.

Not a perfect morning.

Not a bright, easy, fully healed morning.

Just a morning where the concrete in your legs is a little thinner. A morning where the vacuum in your chest is not pulling quite as hard. A morning where the room looks less impossible than it did yesterday.

You wake up, and before you can stop yourself, you notice that something is different.

The ceiling does not feel as far away.

The phone on the nightstand does not look quite as threatening.

The idea of standing up does not immediately feel like being asked to climb a mountain in the dark.

Maybe you get out of bed before noon.

Maybe you open the curtains.

Maybe you answer one message.

Maybe you laugh at something, and the laugh surprises you because it sounds like it came from a version of you that has been missing for a long time.

And then, right behind that tiny relief, the fear comes in.

Does this mean I have to be okay now?

Does this mean people will expect more from me?

Does this mean the dark is gone?

Does this mean I am not allowed to hurt anymore?

A good day can feel beautiful for a moment.

Then it can start to feel like a contract you do not remember signing.

That is why we need to talk about it.

Because good days are not simple when you have lived in the dark for a long time.

They are not always easy.

Sometimes they bring relief.

Sometimes they bring grief.

Sometimes they bring pressure.

Sometimes they bring a strange panic, because you know how quickly the dark can come back. And you may be afraid that everyone around you will treat this one lighter day as proof that the whole nightmare is over.

If that is you, I want you to hear this clearly before we go any further.

A good day is not a contract.

It is a place to breathe.

You do not have to turn one lighter moment into a promise.

You do not have to build a whole future out of one morning where your chest hurt a little less.

You do not have to prove that the darkness is gone just because a small window opened.

You are allowed to receive a good day softly.

You are allowed to let it be only what it is.

A good day.

Not a lifetime agreement.

Not evidence you were never really sick.

Not proof that you owe everyone the old version of yourself back by dinner.

Just a place to breathe.

The Pressure That Follows Relief

When you have been in survival mode for a long time, even relief can feel dangerous.

Part of that danger comes from inside you.

You may feel the old pressure rise almost immediately.

I should use this.

I should catch up.

I should clean the whole house.

I should answer every message.

I should prove I am trying.

I should make up for all the days I lost.

A good day can become a courtroom very quickly.

The voice may begin gathering evidence. It may tell you that if you have a little energy today, you should pay back every unpaid debt of the dark.

Every unanswered text.

Every canceled plan.

Every pile of laundry.

Every postponed task.

Every person you have worried.

Every life you feel like you have been failing to live.

The light comes in, and instead of letting it warm you, you turn it into a spotlight.

You stand under it and begin performing recovery.

You try to make the day impressive enough to prove that you deserved it.

This is one of the quiet traps of a good day.

The day gives you one small breath of space, and the pressure tells you to spend it all at once.

Please do not spend it all at once.

A good day is not a demand to become productive. It is not a command to make up for the dark. It is not a debt collector standing at the foot of your bed with a clipboard.

If you have a little more room inside you today, you do not have to fill every inch of it with obligation.

You can leave some of it empty.

You can let the space exist.

You can practice being in a slightly lighter room without immediately rearranging all the furniture.

This may sound small, but it is not.

Receiving a good day without turning it into pressure is a skill.

It is something you may have to practice slowly.

The smallest version is this:

Just today.

Not, I am better now.

Not, I have to stay this way.

Not, I have to prove something with this.

Just today.

Today has a little more air in it.

That is enough.

When Other People Notice

Sometimes the hardest part of a good day is that other people can see it.

You smile once, and someone says:

It is so good to see you back.

You answer a text, and someone says:

I knew you were doing better.

You come to dinner, take a shower, make a joke, or leave the house for an hour, and suddenly the people who love you relax in a way that makes your chest tighten.

Their relief is understandable.

They have missed you.

They have worried about you.

They have been standing near the dark, trying to understand what they cannot fully enter.

When they see even a little light on your face, they may want to believe the worst is over.

But their relief can become pressure, even when they do not mean for it to.

Because now you may feel responsible for protecting their hope.

You may think:

If I tell them I am still not okay, I will disappoint them.

You may think:

If the dark comes back tomorrow, they will feel like I tricked them.

You may think:

If I let them see this good day, they will expect me to keep having them.

So you begin managing the good day the same way you managed the mask.

You try to look well enough to reassure them, but not so well that they expect too much. You try to enjoy the light without making anyone believe the dark is gone. You try to carry their relief gently, even though you are barely learning how to carry your own.

That is too much weight for one good day.

The people who love you are allowed to feel relieved.

But you are not responsible for turning their relief into a guarantee.

You are allowed to say, even if only to yourself:

This is a good day. It is not a promise.

You may need language for other people too.

Something simple.

Something kind.

Something that protects the truth without inviting a long conversation you may not have energy for.

You could say:

I am grateful today feels a little lighter. I am trying not to put pressure on it.

Or:

Today is better than yesterday, but I still need to take it slowly.

Or:

I am glad to be here. I do not want to turn this into a performance.

You do not have to explain the whole terrain.

You do not have to give a lecture on depression.

You can simply place a small boundary around the good day so it does not become a stage.

A good day deserves protection too.

Not because it is fragile in a hopeless way.

Because it is tender.

Because it is new.

Because light that returns after a long darkness can be sensitive, and sensitivity needs gentleness, not applause so loud it becomes another kind of noise.

The Fear of Losing It

A good day can also hurt because you are afraid to lose it.

You may find yourself watching the day too closely.

Am I still okay?

Is it fading?

Was that the heaviness coming back?

Why did my chest tighten again?

Why am I tired already?

What if this was the only good day I get?

The fear of losing the light can keep you from feeling any of it.

Instead of sitting in the small warmth, you begin guarding it.

Measuring it.

Testing it.

Checking the edges for cracks.

You may become so afraid the dark will return that the fear itself becomes dark.

If that happens, you have not ruined the good day.

You are having a human response to something uncertain.

When you have lived through days that felt endless, your nervous system does not automatically trust relief. It may treat relief like a trick. It may scan for the moment the floor drops out again. It may say, Do not get comfortable. Do not believe this. Do not let your guard down.

That protective response makes sense.

It may not be peaceful, but it makes sense.

You are not ungrateful because you are afraid on a good day.

You are not sabotaging yourself because you do not know how to relax into it.

You are learning how to tolerate a different kind of contrast.

In Book 1, we talked about the splinter of light. We talked about how hope or joy can hurt when it breaks into a place that has been numb for too long. We named the fact that light can feel sharp before it feels warm.

A good day can be a larger version of that splinter.

It is not just a brief laugh or a passing moment of beauty. It is a whole stretch of time where the dark loosens its grip a little.

That can feel wonderful.

It can also feel threatening.

Because if the light is real, then the return of the dark will hurt.

And if the dark returns, the voice may try to use that return as evidence.

See? Nothing lasts.

See? You are back where you started.

See? It was stupid to hope.

This is where we need a new kind of sentence.

The dark returning does not erase the good day.

And the good day does not obligate the dark to stay gone.

Both can be true.

You can have one lighter day, and then a hard day.

You can laugh on Tuesday and cry on Wednesday.

You can feel a little more like yourself for one afternoon and then wake up heavy again.

That does not mean the lighter day was fake.

It does not mean you failed to hold onto it.

It does not mean you are starting over from nothing.

It means recovery is not a straight hallway where every step takes you farther from the dark.

It is more like learning your way through a house with unreliable lights. Some rooms flicker. Some rooms go dark again. Some rooms have a lamp you did not know still worked. Sometimes you find your way back to the same chair and realize that, even there, you know something you did not know before.

You know the matches exist.

You know a window can open.

You know one good day has reached you once, and that matters even if it did not stay.

The Urge to Shut Down a Good Day

There is something else we need to name gently.

Sometimes, when a day starts to feel better, you may feel an urge to shut it down.

You may stay in bed even though you could get up.

You may cancel something you might have enjoyed.

You may pick a fight, doom-scroll, skip the small thing that helps, or return to a familiar numbness because the unfamiliar light feels too exposed.

I want to be very careful here.

This is not blame.

This is not me saying you are choosing depression.

You are not.

This is me saying that sometimes the dark becomes familiar enough that even pain can feel safer than uncertainty.

We talked about that before.

Known pain has a terrible predictability to it. It may be suffocating, but at least you know its shape. A good day has variables. It asks you to risk wanting something. It asks you to feel the possibility of disappointment. It asks you to stand near the door and admit that part of you may still want to leave the dark room.

That can be terrifying.

So if you notice yourself pulling back from a good day, try not to attack yourself for it.

Try to name it softly.

This is the part of me that is afraid of hope.

This is the part of me that does not want to be dropped again.

This is the part of me that trusts the dark because the dark is familiar.

Naming it this way creates a little room.

Not a lecture.

Not a punishment.

A little room.

And in that room, you can choose one small way to stay near the good day without forcing yourself to become bright.

You do not have to run into the sunlight.

You can sit near the window.

You can let the curtain stay half closed.

You can let the room be gray.

You can say:

Just today, I will not punish myself for feeling a little better.

That may be the whole practice.

How to Receive a Good Day Softly

A good day does not need to be used aggressively.

It can be received.

That word matters.

Received.

Not conquered.

Not proven.

Not maximized.

Not converted into a productivity sprint.

If the day gives you a little more air, you can let yourself breathe some of it before you decide what to do with it.

Here are a few ways to practice that.

You can choose one pleasure.

Not a huge celebration. Not a full schedule. Just one small thing that does not need to justify itself.

A warm drink.

A clean shirt.

A song you used to love.

A few minutes outside.

A favorite blanket without apologizing for resting under it.

A good day does not have to be spent only on catching up. Some of it can be spent on remembering that you are allowed to receive comfort.

You can choose one clean signal.

If there is a practical thing that would make tomorrow slightly easier, choose one.

Not ten.

Not the whole list.

One.

Start the laundry, but do not require yourself to finish every basket.

Wash the cup by the bed, but do not turn the kitchen into a test of your worth.

Take a shower, but do not decide that showering means you now owe the world a full performance of wellness.

One signal.

One closed loop.

Then stop if stopping is wise.

You can choose one breath.

Even on a good day, your body may still be bracing. You may still be waiting for the drop. You may still be scanning for danger.

So take one breath and step back.

Name what is happening.

This is a better day.

I am afraid it will not last.

I do not have to solve that fear right now.

That is enough.

You can choose one gentle boundary.

Maybe you do not tell everyone you are doing better.

Maybe you do not accept every invitation.

Maybe you say yes to lunch but no to the rest of the day.

Maybe you tell someone:

I want to enjoy this without making it bigger than it is.

A good day does not remove your right to have limits.

You are allowed to protect the light from becoming pressure.

You can choose one safe room.

Even if you feel lighter, you may still need somewhere inside you where the dark does not get every chair. You can visit that room before the day becomes too loud. You can sit there for a moment and remind yourself that you do not have to earn peace by being impressive.

The tools we have been building do not disappear on good days.

They may become even more important.

Because good days can tempt you to abandon gentleness.

They can make you think:

I have energy, so I should spend all of it.

The tools remind you to stay small enough to stay safe.

Splinter.

The voice.

One signal.

One breath.

Safe room.

Just today.

These are not rules.

They are handles.

And on a good day, you are allowed to hold one.

The Good Day Does Not Erase the Dark

Sometimes you may feel guilty for having a good day.

That sounds strange until you have lived it.

You may wonder if feeling better for a few hours means you were exaggerating before.

You may think:

If I can laugh today, why couldn't I answer that message last week?

You may think:

If I can go outside today, why couldn't I do it yesterday?

You may look back at the worst days with suspicion, as if the existence of one good day puts all your suffering on trial.

It does not.

A good day does not prove the dark was fake.

It proves the dark is not the only thing that can reach you.

That is very different.

Illness can fluctuate.

Pain can fluctuate.

Energy can fluctuate.

Capacity can fluctuate.

You are allowed to have a lighter day without retroactively accusing yourself of lying about the heavy ones.

You are allowed to enjoy one hour without explaining why you could not enjoy the last hundred.

You are allowed to be inconsistent because healing is often inconsistent.

The good day is not here to prosecute the dark days.

It is here to give you a little room.

Let it be room.

Let it be breath.

Let it be a candle without demanding that it become the sun.

When the Dark Comes Back

If the dark comes back after a good day, the voice may get loud.

It may say you lost your progress.

It may say you failed.

It may say you should have known better than to hope.

It may say the good day was a trick.

This is when you may need to be very gentle and very firm with the voice.

You can say:

The good day was real.

This hard day is real too.

One does not erase the other.

Then shrink the timeline again.

Not forever.

Not recovery.

Not the whole future.

Just today.

What is the next smallest honest thing?

Maybe it is water.

Maybe it is soap.

Maybe it is texting one safe person:

The dark is loud today.

Maybe it is opening the curtains for one minute and closing them again.

Maybe it is returning to the safe room inside you and sitting in the chair the dark does not get.

Maybe it is calling or texting 988 if the voice starts telling you that you should not be here, that people would be better off without you, or that you might hurt yourself.

A good day does not remove the need for safety.

And a hard day after a good day does not mean you are hopeless.

It means the terrain is uneven.

You are still walking.

Even if today you are walking by staying in place.

Even if today the only movement is asking someone else to stand beside you until the worst of the wave passes.

That still counts.

Late practice still counts.

A good day that ends still counts.

A hard day after a good day still counts.

You still count.

For Today

If today is a good day, you do not have to turn it into proof.

You do not have to promise anyone that you will feel this way tomorrow.

You do not have to spend all your energy catching up, reassuring people, or performing recovery.

You can receive one lighter moment softly.

You can choose one pleasure, one clean signal, one breath, one gentle boundary, or one quiet visit to the safe room inside you.

You can let the day be what it is without making it responsible for the rest of your life.

And if the dark comes back later, that does not mean the good day was fake.

It only means the good day was a place you visited.

A place can matter even if you do not live there yet.

For today, you can say:

A good day is not a contract.

It is a place to breathe.

Just today.

That is enough.

You do not have to become the sun.

You can simply let one window stay open for as long as it can.

And if you need to close it again, you are still worthy of care.

You are still here.

That still matters.

Chapter 7: When the Tools Fail

When Nothing Changes

There is a particular kind of heartbreak that happens when you finally try the thing.

Not when you avoid it.

Not when you cannot make yourself begin.

When you actually try.

You take the breath. You name the voice. You look for one clean signal. You sit in the room you have been building in your mind. You reach for the tool this book handed you, and for one small moment, some part of you hopes it might help.

Maybe not fix everything.

Maybe not lift the whole dark.

But help.

Just a little.

You do the thing as best you can, and then you wait for the shift.

The chest is still heavy.

The room is still impossible.

The voice is still loud.

The light still hurts.

Nothing in you opens. Nothing softens. Nothing feels rescued.

And then the shame comes in fast.

I could not even do this.

That sentence can land harder than the original pain.

Before the tool, you were just hurting. After the tool does not work, the voice may try to turn your pain into evidence. It may say, See? Even this was too much for you. Even the small thing was too hard. Even the gentlest instruction was beyond you.

That is a cruel place to stand.

It is also a place we need to name carefully, because this book has spent several chapters offering you small handles.

Splinter.

The voice.

One signal.

One breath.

Safe room.

Just today.

Those handles are meant to give you something to reach for when the dark gets too thick.

They are not meant to become another set of expectations that can be used against you.

A tool failing is not the same as you failing.

I want that sentence to sit very plainly in the room.

A tool failing is not the same as you failing.

If you tried something and it did not help, that does not mean you did it wrong. It does not mean you are too broken for help. It does not mean you are secretly unwilling to heal. It does not mean you have disappointed this book, yourself, God, your family, your therapist, your medication, your future, or anyone else who has ever wanted you to be okay.

It means one tool, in one moment, under one set of conditions, was not enough.

That is information.

It is not a verdict.

The Shame After Trying

Shame loves to arrive right after effort.

It waits until you have used the little bit of strength you had, and then it tries to punish you for not producing a miracle.

You finally stand in the bathroom and turn on the shower, but the sound of the water makes you want to cry. You sit on the edge of the tub, wrapped in a towel, unable to step in.

The voice says:

You cannot even take a shower.

You try to create the Voice Gap, but the thought comes too fast and too loud. You know you are supposed to say, That is the voice, but the sentence will not form.

The voice says:

You cannot even notice me.

You close your eyes and try to go to your safe room, but your mind will not cooperate. The door will not appear. The blanket will not feel real. The room feels far away, like a place you invented for someone stronger than you.

The voice says:

You cannot even imagine safety.

You wake up on a good day and try to receive it softly, but the pressure comes anyway. You start counting all the things you should do while the light is available, and by noon you are exhausted and angry.

The voice says:

You cannot even enjoy relief.

Do you hear the pattern?

The voice is not simply commenting on the tool.

It is using the tool as a weapon.

That is not what these tools are for.

They are not tests of character.

They are not proof of discipline.

They are not little moral exams hidden inside gentle language.

They are not a way for you to earn care by showing that you are trying hard enough.

You do not have to become a perfect user of coping skills in order to be worthy of compassion.

You do not have to perform recovery correctly.

You do not have to make the people who love you feel better by being good at the tools.

There may be days when the only true sentence is this:

I tried, and it did not help.

That sentence is allowed to exist without becoming an accusation.

It can be true without meaning you are hopeless.

It can be true without meaning the tools are useless.

It can be true without meaning you have gone backward.

It can simply mean that today was heavier than the tool you reached for.

Tools Are Not Proof of Worth

One of the quiet dangers of practical help is that it can become another place to measure yourself.

When you were only reading about the dark, you may have felt seen. But once a book starts offering tools, a frightened part of you may begin keeping score.

Did I use it?

Did I use it right?

Did it work fast enough?

Did I make progress?

That scorekeeping can turn even gentle practices into pressure. It can make a breath feel like homework. It can make a shower feel like a performance. It can make a safe room feel like a place you have failed to enter properly.

So let us be very clear.

The purpose of a tool is to serve you.

Your purpose is not to serve the tool.

If a tool helps you, we honor that.

If a tool does not help you, we listen to that.

If a tool helped yesterday but does not help today, we do not accuse you of inconsistency.

We recognize that the terrain changed.

Depression is not a neat problem. A human nervous system is not a machine that responds the same way every time someone pushes the same button.

You are not a machine.

You are a person.

A person can have a day when hot water feels soothing and another day when hot water feels like too much sensation.

A person can have a day when naming the voice creates space and another day when the voice is too loud to name.

That variation is not failure.

It is humanity.

It is weather.

It is the simple truth that you are alive inside changing conditions, not completing a worksheet in a quiet room with unlimited energy.

A tool can be good and still not be the right tool for this minute.

A tool can be gentle and still be too large for this hour.

A tool can be useful and still need to be put down.

None of that says anything about your worth.

Your worth was never hanging on whether you could take a shower, answer a text, breathe deeply, eat something, pray, journal, stretch, go outside, or think the correct thought at the correct time.

Your worth is not that fragile.

Failure Is Information

When something does not work, the voice wants to call it a verdict.

The gentler response is to call it information.

A verdict says:

This proves who you are.

Information says:

This tells us something about what is happening.

Those are very different rooms.

A verdict closes the door.

Information opens a window.

If the shower is too much, that may be information that your body is overstimulated, depleted, or afraid of the sequence of steps. It may be information that the tool needs to become smaller.

If the Voice Gap is too hard, that may be information that the voice is extremely loud today. It may mean you do not have the energy to create a whole sentence around the thought. It may mean you need someone else to help you remember what is true. It may mean the tool needs to shrink down to one phrase.

The voice.

That may be enough.

If the safe room is inaccessible, that may be information that your imagination is tired. It may mean your body needs a physical object instead of a mental picture. It may mean that the blanket on your bed, the texture of your sleeve, or the cool side of the pillow is the safest door available right now.

If a good day becomes pressure, that may be information that you are not ready to spend the relief. It may mean the light needs to stay small. It may mean the best use of a good day is not productivity, but protection.

Information does not shame you.

It adjusts the next step.

That is all.

You do not have to stand over a failed tool and punish yourself until it starts working.

You do not have to prove your sincerity by repeating an action that is overwhelming you.

You are allowed to notice:

This is not helping right now.

You are allowed to change the size.

You are allowed to change the tool.

You are allowed to ask for help.

You are allowed to rest.

This is where the smallest version of this chapter comes in.

Try softer.

Not harder.

Softer.

Try Softer

Trying softer is not giving up.

It is refusing to turn healing into a fight against yourself.

So much of life teaches us that when something does not work, the answer is more force.

Try harder.

Push through.

Be disciplined.

Stop making excuses.

Dig deep.

Power forward.

There may be places in life where that language makes sense.

The dark is usually not one of them.

When you are already carrying the hundred-pound backpack no one else can see, more force may not free you. It may drive you deeper into collapse. It may make the tool feel like another person standing over you with crossed arms, waiting to see if you are finally going to get yourself together.

Trying softer means asking a different question.

Not:

How do I make myself do this?

But:

How small does this need to become before my body can touch it?

Not:

Why am I so bad at this?

But:

What is this failed attempt telling me?

Not:

How do I prove I am trying?

But:

What would help me stay with myself without adding shame?

Trying softer may mean making the tool smaller.

The shower is too much, so you wash your hands.

You do not make the water perfect. You do not turn it into a ritual. You do not demand that handwashing become the first step toward a full hygiene routine.

You just put your hands under the water and let soap touch skin.

One clean signal.

Smaller.

Still real.

Trying softer may mean changing tools.

Breath and Step Back is too hard because focusing on your breath makes you feel trapped in your body. So instead of taking a deep breath, you look across the room and name one ordinary object.

Lamp.

Door.

Shoe.

Blanket.

You are not doing the formal tool.

You are finding the edge of it by touching one plain thing in the room.

Trying softer may mean asking for help.

You cannot make food. You cannot decide what sounds good. Every option feels too hard. So you text someone, if you can, and say:

Could you bring me something simple?

You do not need to explain your whole condition.

You do not need to prove you deserve the help.

If the person is safe and available, letting another human being do one practical thing is not a failure of independence.

It is a form of staying here.

Trying softer may mean resting.

Not collapsing in shame.

Resting.

There is a difference.

Shame says:

I am going back to bed because I am useless.

Rest says:

I am going back to bed because my body is overwhelmed, and forcing this tool right now will cost more than it gives.

The outside action may look the same.

The room inside it is different.

Trying softer protects that room.

When the Tool Needs to Become Tiny

Let us make this very ordinary, because ordinary is where these tools have to live.

If the shower is too much, wash your hands.

If washing your hands is too much, touch the soap bottle.

If touching the soap bottle is too much, look toward the bathroom door and tell the truth:

Not yet.

Not never.

Not proof that you are hopeless.

Not yet.

If One Clean Signal is too much as a full action, find one clean signal that is smaller than the one you planned. Put on clean socks. Rinse a cup. Throw away one tissue. Open the curtains one inch. Put your feet on the floor for ten seconds and then get back into bed.

The point is not to impress anyone.

The point is to create one honest mark in reality that says:

I touched the world.

If the Voice Gap is too hard, do not try to write a speech against the voice. Do not try to prove that the thought is false. Do not try to become your own defense attorney when you are exhausted.

Just say:

The voice.

If even that is too much, shorten it further.

Voice.

That one word can be a thread.

It may not silence the thought. It may not make you believe something better. It may not change the feeling in your chest.

But it can mark the thought as something happening, not the whole of who you are.

If the safe room is inaccessible, stop trying to force the room to appear.

Touch the blanket.

Let the blanket be the room for today.

Feel one corner of it between your fingers. Notice whether it is soft, rough, heavy, cool, warm, familiar, or simply there. You do not have to imagine walls. You do not have to find a door. You do not have to create a perfect shelter inside your mind.

Safe room.

Smaller.

A texture.

A corner.

A hand on fabric.

If Just today is too large, because even one day feels like too long, shrink the timeline again.

Just this hour.

Just this minute.

Just this breath, if breath feels safe.

Just this blanket.

Just this page.

Just the next sip of water.

Trying softer lets the tool come down to the size of the life you are actually living, not the life someone else thinks you should be able to manage.

When Rest Is the Tool

Sometimes the tool fails because it was the wrong tool.

Sometimes the tool fails because you are too depleted for any tool that asks something of you.

That matters.

There are days when every coping skill feels like a demand.

Even gentle ones.

On those days, the next right move may be rest.

Not as avoidance.

Not as punishment.

Not as proof that the dark won.

Rest as a tool.

Rest can be an active choice to stop spending energy on self-attack. Rest can be the moment you decide not to rehearse the entire list of what you did not do. Rest can be letting the body lie down without turning the bed into a courtroom.

This is harder than it sounds.

When you are depressed, resting rarely feels clean. It often comes covered in guilt. You may be lying still, but inside your mind, you are dragging yourself through a trial.

You should be up.

You should be better.

You should be stronger.

You should be using the tools.

What if, for today, rest was not the place you went because the tools failed?

What if rest was the tool that came next?

Rest does not mean doing nothing inside yourself.

Rest may mean refusing to add another layer of injury.

Rest may mean placing one hand on the blanket and saying:

I am allowed to stop for a while.

You may not feel peaceful when you say it.

That is okay.

Peace is not required.

Permission can come before peace.

You can rest while still feeling sad.

You can rest while still feeling frustrated.

You can rest while still wishing the tool had worked.

You can rest while not being proud of yourself yet.

Rest does not need your approval to count.

When the Next Tool Is Another Human Being

There is one place where we need to be very clear.

If the tools are failing because you are unsafe, the next tool is not a smaller exercise.

The next tool is another human being.

If the voice is telling you that everyone would be better off without you, if you might hurt yourself, if you do not trust yourself to stay alive, or if the gap between the thought and believing it has disappeared, please do not keep trying to handle that alone.

Call or text 988 if you are in the United States.

You do not have to have the right words.

You do not have to explain your whole story.

You can say:

I am not safe by myself right now.

You can say:

The voice is telling me I should not be here.

If 988 is not available where you are, contact your local emergency number, crisis line, or a safe person who can physically be with you or help you get immediate support.

This is not you failing the tools.

This is you choosing the correct tool for the level of danger.

A book is not enough for that moment.

A breathing exercise is not enough for that moment.

A safe room in your mind is not enough for that moment if your body is in danger.

Another human being is the tool.

Let someone else stand between you and the voice for a little while.

Let someone else hold the line when your hands are too tired.

That is not weakness.

That is survival.

And survival is the work.

You Are Still Allowed to Need Help

One reason tool failure can feel so humiliating is that you may already be tired of needing help.

You may be tired of having to think this hard about ordinary things. Tired of turning showers into strategies. Tired of turning thoughts into voices. Tired of turning rest into permission.

It makes sense if you are tired.

It makes sense if part of you wants to say:

I do not want another coping skill. I want a life that does not require this much coping.

That is a fair grief.

We do not need to spiritualize it or brighten it.

It is exhausting to need tools for survival.

It is exhausting to learn gentleness after living under an inner voice that has been prosecuting you for years.

If you resent the tools sometimes, that does not make you ungrateful.

If you are bored by them, that does not make you careless.

If you forget them, that does not make you hopeless.

If you try them and they do not work, that does not make you the problem.

It makes you a human being in a hard room.

This book is not here to stand at the front of that room and grade you.

It is here to sit beside you and offer handles when handles are useful.

When they are not useful, we make them smaller.

When smaller does not help, we change tools.

When changing tools is too much, we rest.

When rest is not safe enough, we bring in another human being.

At no point do we turn on you.

That is the rule.

At no point do we turn on you.

The Soft Return

There may come a moment, later, when a tool that failed before becomes available again.

The shower that was impossible on Monday may become a hand wash on Tuesday.

The Voice Gap that vanished in the morning may return for two seconds at night.

The safe room that would not appear may come back as only a blanket, then a corner, then a room.

A good day that became pressure this week may become a place to breathe next week.

You do not have to force that return.

You do not have to stand guard over yourself, waiting to catch the exact minute when you are capable again.

Capability often returns shyly.

It may not announce itself as strength. It may look like reaching for water, opening a message and not answering it yet, noticing the voice after believing it for three hours, or asking someone to sit with you without advice.

These are not small things because they are easy.

They are small because they are sized for survival.

If a tool failed today, you do not have to decide what that means about tomorrow.

You do not have to make a prophecy out of a hard morning.

You do not have to say:

This never works.

You can say:

This did not work right now.

That little phrase leaves the door unlocked.

Right now.

Not forever.

Right now.

It gives you permission to stop without declaring the whole path closed.

It lets you put the tool down gently instead of throwing it away in shame.

And if later does not come today, that is not a verdict either.

It is information.

Try softer.

For Today

For today, if a tool does not work, do not use it as evidence against yourself.

A tool failing is not the same as you failing.

You may make it smaller.

You may change tools.

You may ask for help.

You may rest.

If the shower is too much, wash your hands.

If the Voice Gap is too hard, say only:

The voice.

If the safe room feels far away, touch the blanket.

If one day is too long, try one minute.

And if you are unsafe, let the next tool be another human being. Call or text 988 if you might hurt yourself or cannot stay alone with the voice.

You do not have to try harder today.

Try softer.

Stay with yourself.

Do not turn on yourself.

That may be enough for today.

Chapter 8: The Slow Return of Color

When the World Is Gray

There is a kind of gray that is more than a color.

It is a weather inside the body.

It is the morning light coming through the window and not reaching you. It is food that has texture but no invitation. It is music playing somewhere in the background while your mind registers only noise. It is a room full of objects you used to like, all of them sitting there quietly, unable to call you back.

The world may still have color in it.

Technically.

The blanket is still blue.

The mug is still yellow.

The leaves outside are still green.

Someone may still be laughing in the next room. The soap may still smell like lavender or citrus or something clean and ordinary.

But inside the dark, none of it lands.

It is not that beauty disappears from the world. It is that beauty cannot get through the thick glass between you and everything else.

You can see it, maybe.

You can name it.

You can understand that another version of you might have cared.

But caring is far away.

You may remember being the kind of person who noticed things.

A good sky.

A song lyric.

The smell of rain on pavement.

A soft sweater.

A ridiculous dog.

The first sip of coffee.

A color in a shop window.

Someone's laugh from across a room.

You may remember that person and feel almost embarrassed by them.

How did they have room for all that?

How did they move through a world that kept offering little pleasures and actually receive them?

When you are deep in the dark, those small openings can feel unavailable.

Not because you are ungrateful.

Not because you are cold.

Not because you are refusing life.

The receiving part of you may simply be exhausted.

That is real.

And because it is real, we are not going to begin this chapter by demanding that you become bright.

We are not going to ask you to celebrate.

We are not going to ask you to look on the bright side.

We are not going to hand you a gratitude list and tell you to prove that you still know how to be a person.

We are going to begin much smaller than that.

We are going to talk about the slow return of color.

Not a sunrise.

Not a transformation.

Not a promise that everything is better now.

A little color.

Hope Does Not Have to Be Loud

When people talk about hope, they often make it sound enormous.

They make it sound like standing on a mountain with your arms open. They make it sound like a worship song at full volume. They make it sound like a before-and-after picture where the old life falls away and the new life arrives clean, radiant, and easy to explain.

That kind of hope may exist for some people in some moments.

But it is not the only kind.

There is also quiet hope.

There is hope so small you might not even call it hope while it is happening.

You smell toast and, for half a second, it smells good.

You see the edge of the sky turning pink and something in you notices before the numbness closes again.

You hear a song you used to love and one line finds its way through.

You choose the green shirt instead of the gray one, not because you are becoming a new person, but because for one strange second, green feels possible.

You laugh once.

Not all day.

Not freely.

Not the way you used to.

Just once, before your own laugh surprises you.

You reach for a blanket and realize the texture feels comforting.

You take a sip of cold water and it tastes clean.

That is not nothing.

It may feel like nothing because it does not fix the whole room. It does not pay the bills. It does not answer the hard texts. It does not erase grief. It does not make the voice disappear. It does not mean tomorrow will be easy.

But it is still something.

Color can return slowly and still be real.

Let that sentence stay small.

Color can return slowly and still be real.

The dark may want to dismiss anything that does not arrive as rescue.

It may say:

If this were real, it would last.

If this mattered, it would change everything.

If you were really healing, you would feel better for more than three seconds.

But the dark has always been a bad judge of small things.

A seed does not look like a garden.

A match does not look like morning.

A single note does not look like a whole song.

And a small moment of color does not have to look like full recovery in order to matter.

It only has to be what it is.

A little color.

The First Color May Feel Strange

The first returning color may not feel like joy.

That is important.

Sometimes people expect healing to feel good immediately. They imagine that when life begins to reach them again, the relief will be clean and simple. They imagine a door opening. Air entering. Light landing softly on the face.

Sometimes that happens.

Sometimes it does not.

Sometimes the first color hurts.

You notice a smell and suddenly remember how long it has been since anything smelled good. You laugh and then feel grief rise up behind it because you realize how long your laugh has been gone. You see something beautiful and feel an ache so sharp it almost feels like punishment.

Why does that hurt?

Because color returning can show you what gray has taken.

It can make the absence visible.

When the world has been muted for a long time, the first bright thing may not feel gentle. It may feel too sharp. It may make you want to close your eyes again.

Not because you hate beauty.

Because beauty has touched a tender place.

That tenderness is not failure.

It is not ingratitude.

It is not proof that you are too damaged to receive good things.

It may simply be grief.

You are allowed to grieve when color returns.

You are allowed to feel sad that a smell used to reach you easily and now arrives like a visitor from another life. You are allowed to miss the version of you who could enjoy a song without analyzing whether the enjoyment meant something. You are allowed to feel both grateful and heartbroken when one small preference comes back.

I want to say that plainly because some people will misunderstand this part.

They will see a small sign of life in you and immediately celebrate so loudly that the sign retreats.

They will say:

See, you are getting better.

They will want the moment to become proof, momentum, a turning point, a story they can hold onto because they are tired of being scared for you.

They may mean well.

But the moment may not be ready to carry that much weight.

A little color is not a contract.

It is not a promise that you will stay brighter.

It is not an agreement that you are now available for everyone else's relief.

It is only a sign.

A real sign.

A small sign.

A sign that something in you can still be reached.

That is enough.

Do Not Chase It

When color appears, you may feel pressure to grab it.

This is understandable.

If you have been living in gray for a long time, even a small flash can feel precious. You may want to keep it from leaving. You may want to build a system around it. You may want to repeat whatever caused it, just in case that is the doorway.

The song made me feel something.

Should I listen to it again?

Should I make a playlist?

Should I become a person who listens to music every morning?

The tea tasted good.

Should I buy five kinds of tea?

Should I fix my whole routine?

Should I become someone who has peaceful evenings now?

I laughed at that video.

Should I send it to someone?

Should I explain that I laughed?

Should I prove that I am still fun?

Pressure can arrive even inside a good moment.

It can turn color into homework.

So here is the gentler instruction.

Do not chase it.

Notice it if you can.

Let it visit.

Let it leave.

This may sound too passive if you are used to fighting for every inch of survival. But sometimes chasing a small sign of life is the very thing that scares it away. The receiving part of you may still be fragile. It may need gentleness more than effort.

Think of a bird landing near you.

If you lunge toward it, it flies.

If you stay still, it may stay for one second longer.

Color can be like that at first.

Not because it is weak.

Because you are tender.

You do not have to prove that you noticed it correctly.

You do not have to make a lesson out of it.

You do not have to turn it into a plan.

If the smell of coffee reaches you for half a second, you can let that be the whole thing.

Coffee.

Warm.

Here.

If the blanket feels soft, you can let that be the whole thing.

Soft.

Mine.

Enough.

If a color catches your eye, you can let that be the whole thing.

Blue.

Bright.

A little color.

The smallest version of this chapter is not a command to become hopeful.

It is not even:

Find the color.

It is only this:

A little color.

That is small enough.

How Color Returns

Color usually returns through ordinary doors.

Not always.

But often.

It may return through the body before it returns through belief.

A smell.

A texture.

A temperature.

A taste.

A sound.

Something very plain may reach you before a large emotional truth does.

This is why the previous tools matter, even when they seem small.

One Clean Signal may help color return for a moment.

You wash your hands because the shower is too much, and the soap smells sharp and clean. You do not become happy. You do not become fixed. But for one second, there is a smell other than stale air and fear.

That counts.

Breath and Step Back may help you notice without turning the moment into a whole story.

You hear a song through a passing car window. A line catches in your chest. The voice starts to say, This only proves what you lost. You take one breath and step back far enough to say:

A song reached me for a second.

That counts.

The Voice Gap may help you protect the color from the voice.

The voice says, If you can enjoy that, then you are not really depressed.

Or it says:

If you were really getting better, this would last.

You notice:

That is the voice.

You do not have to argue. You only create enough room for the small thing to remain small.

That counts.

The good day tool may help you avoid spending the color as soon as it arrives.

You wake up and the room feels less heavy. The pressure says, Use it. Prove it. Catch up. Fix the whole life. But you remember that a good day does not have to become a performance. You let one window open without turning the whole house into a project.

That counts.

And if a tool failed yesterday, that does not erase the color that appears today.

A failed tool does not cancel a small sign of life.

You can have a hard morning and still notice the smell of rain in the afternoon.

You can cry in the shower and still feel the clean towel afterward.

You can be unable to answer a text and still see the way sunlight lands on the floor.

The dark may want everything to be consistent before it counts. It may want a perfect pattern. It may want evidence that your healing is orderly, dependable, and easy to chart.

But life returning is often uneven.

A little color here.

Gray again.

A small laugh.

Quiet again.

One clean taste of water.

Heavy again.

This unevenness is not proof that the color was fake.

It is proof that you are still in a changing place.

When Color Scares You

Sometimes color returning can feel dangerous.

Not because the color itself is dangerous, but because hope can feel like a setup.

If you have hoped before and been disappointed, a small sign of life may make you flinch. If you have had a good hour followed by a terrible night, you may not trust the good hour. If you have watched relief vanish before you could hold it, you may feel suspicious when relief comes near again.

Of course you might.

You are not being cynical for protecting yourself.

You are remembering pain.

The dark may be cruel, but it is familiar. Gray may be miserable, but it is predictable. Color introduces uncertainty. If something good can reach you, then something can also be lost. If a preference comes back, then you can miss it when it leaves. If a laugh returns, then the silence afterward may feel louder.

This is why we are keeping the hope quiet.

We are not asking you to open every curtain.

We are not asking you to trust the whole future.

We are not asking you to announce that things are better.

We are only asking whether, for one second, something had a color.

That is all.

You can be afraid and still notice.

You can distrust the moment and still let it be real.

You can say:

I do not know what this means.

You can say:

I am scared to want anything.

You can say:

I liked that for half a second, and I do not know what to do with that.

You do not have to know what to do with it.

You do not have to turn it into a decision.

You do not have to defend it in court.

At no point do we turn on you.

Not when the world is gray.

Not when color returns.

Not when color hurts.

Not when color leaves again.

A Sign Is Not a Demand

A small sign of life can be mishandled if we turn it into a demand.

This is where many people, including the people who love you, may need to learn a gentler way.

If you laugh once, it does not mean you are ready to socialize.

If you enjoy one meal, it does not mean food is easy now.

If you notice that the sky is beautiful, it does not mean you owe anyone a cheerful afternoon.

If you have one lighter hour, it does not mean the dark was exaggerated.

If you say, I think I might want to sit outside, it does not mean someone should immediately plan a whole day in the sun.

A sign is not a demand.

A sign is not a contract.

A sign is not a performance review.

A sign is not proof that you have to keep improving at the same speed.

A sign is only a sign.

It may point to life.

It may point to capacity.

It may point to a place where the numbness thinned for a second.

But it does not get to become a leash.

If color returns for a moment, you are allowed to receive it without promising anything.

You are allowed to say, That was nice, and then lie down.

You are allowed to say, I liked that smell, and still be sad.

You are allowed to say, The blue looked beautiful, and still not know how to answer your messages.

You are allowed to let one small sign be one small sign.

This is how we protect hope from becoming pressure.

We keep it honest.

We keep it small.

We keep it kind.

Color can return slowly and still be real.

It can also return briefly and still be real.

It can return unevenly and still be real.

It can return with grief beside it and still be real.

Let the Color Be Small

There may be a day when you notice something.

A red leaf.

A clean pillowcase.

The smell of toast.

The exact comfort of warm socks.

A song lyric that does not fix you but finds you.

A tiny preference.

Not this cup.

That one.

Not that blanket.

This one.

Not silence.

Maybe the soft song.

A preference can be a small miracle when you have been living without wanting anything.

It does not have to be dramatic.

It may even be annoying.

You may think:

Really? This is what comes back first? A preference about mugs?

Yes.

Maybe.

Let it be that ordinary.

The dark often makes life feel abstract and impossible. It turns everything into large questions.

What is the point?

Will I always feel this way?

Who am I now?

How do I build a future from a body this tired?

Those questions are too big for most days.

Color returns in smaller grammar.

This smells good.

That feels soft.

I like blue.

The air is cool.

The dog is funny.

This page is still here.

These sentences may sound almost childlike.

Good.

Let them be simple.

Let them exist before analysis arrives.

Let them be small enough to hold.

A little color.

That is the practice.

Not hunting beauty.

Not proving hope.

Not forcing gratitude.

Only allowing one small true thing to be true.

For Today

For today, do not ask yourself to become bright.

Do not ask yourself to become hopeful in a way other people can recognize.

Do not ask one small sign of life to carry the whole future.

If the world feels gray, tell the truth.

The world feels gray today.

If one small thing reaches you, tell the truth about that too.

A little color.

Maybe it is a smell.

Maybe it is a sound.

Maybe it is the blue of a mug, the softness of a blanket, the first clean sip of water, the way light touches the floor, or a tiny laugh that surprises you.

You do not have to chase it.

You do not have to keep it.

You do not have to make it mean more than it means.

You can simply notice:

Something reached me for a second.

If noticing color hurts because it reminds you of how long things have been gray, be gentle with that grief.

The hurt does not cancel the color.

The color does not cancel the hurt.

Both can sit in the room.

If the voice tries to turn the moment into pressure, you can name it.

The voice.

If the pressure says, Now you have to stay better, you can answer softly.

Not today.

If the color leaves again, you have not failed.

A sign is not a contract.

A little color is enough for today.

Color can return slowly and still be real.

A little color.

Chapter 9: You Are Still Here

When Survival Does Not Feel Triumphant

There are days when staying alive does not feel brave.

It may not feel like courage.

It may not feel like strength.

It may not feel like anything you would ever put on a poster or say out loud with your hand over your heart.

It may feel like lying in the same bed, in the same room, under the same blanket, listening to the same thoughts circle the same tired places in your mind.

It may feel like getting through another night because the night passed, not because you defeated it.

It may feel like waking up disappointed to still be waking up.

It may feel like being here only because something in you did not know how to leave.

If that is where you are, I am not going to ask you to call it triumph.

I am not going to dress your survival in language that feels too shiny for the room you are in.

You do not have to feel proud in order for your staying to matter.

You do not have to feel inspired in order for your life to be worth protecting.

You do not have to feel strong in order to have done something difficult.

Sometimes survival is not a raised fist.

Sometimes survival is a hand still resting on the blanket.

Sometimes it is one breath you did not know you were still taking.

Sometimes it is not choosing the worst thing in the worst minute.

Sometimes it is simply this:

You are still here.

And I want to say the next part gently, without making it heavy.

You are still here, and that matters.

Not because you have solved everything.

Not because you are suddenly ready.

Not because the dark has lifted or the voice has gone quiet or the bridge is finished.

It matters because you matter.

Even here.

Especially here.

Still Here Is Not Small

The phrase can sound almost plain.

Still here.

Two little words.

They do not announce themselves. They do not explain the whole story. They do not tell anyone how hard the night was or how much work it took to keep your body in the world for one more day.

But plain things can be holy.

A cup of water.

A clean towel.

A closed door.

A hand on a shoulder.

A breath.

Still here.

If you have lived with the dark long enough, you know that staying is not automatic.

People who have never been that tired may not understand this. They may think being alive is the default setting, and anything else is an emergency that begins suddenly.

But sometimes the emergency is not sudden.

Sometimes the emergency is quiet and long.

Sometimes it is the slow wearing down of your ability to imagine tomorrow. Sometimes it is the voice repeating the same lie so often that you stop feeling shocked by it. Sometimes it is a grayness so complete that even the idea of wanting to live feels like a language you used to know.

So if you are still here, that is not nothing.

It may not feel like victory.

It may not feel like healing.

It may not feel like hope.

But it is a fact the dark did not erase.

You remained.

Maybe with help.

Maybe barely.

Maybe angrily.

Maybe numb.

Maybe because someone sat with you.

Maybe because you called.

Maybe because you texted.

Maybe because you promised a person, a pet, a child, a future appointment, or one stubborn corner of yourself that you would wait until morning.

However you stayed, you stayed.

That matters.

We Are Not Making You a Warrior

There is a way people sometimes talk about suffering that can become its own kind of pressure.

They call you a warrior.

They call you brave.

They call you inspiring.

They say you are so strong, and maybe they mean it with love. Maybe they are trying to honor what they can see. Maybe they need language big enough to hold how scared they have been for you.

But sometimes those words can feel like another costume.

What if you do not feel like a warrior?

What if you do not want to be inspirational?

What if you are tired of being strong?

What if the most honest thing you can say is:

I am still here, but I am so tired.

Then we will not argue with you.

We will not force a medal into your hands and ask you to smile for the picture.

We will not turn your pain into a lesson for other people.

We will not require you to feel noble about something that has cost you so much.

Dignity is not the same as performance.

You can have dignity without feeling brave.

You can have dignity while crying.

You can have dignity while needing help.

You can have dignity while being angry that this is your fight at all.

You can have dignity while not knowing whether you want to keep going.

Your dignity does not depend on your mood, your productivity, your posture, your ability to explain yourself, or your capacity to make other people comfortable with your pain.

Your dignity belongs to you because you are a person.

Still here.

Still worthy.

Still not a problem to be solved before you can be loved.

The Bridge Has Boards Now

When this book began, we were not trying to build a whole bridge in one day.

That would have been cruel.

The dark was too heavy for grand plans. The light was too sharp for easy hope. The voice was too convincing for simple reassurance. The body was too tired for big instructions.

So we reached for small things.

A splinter.

The voice.

One signal.

One breath.

Safe room.

Just today.

Try softer.

A little color.

None of these were meant to fix everything.

They were never meant to become proof that you are healing correctly. They were never meant to make you impressive. They were never meant to turn your pain into a neat little progress chart.

They were boards.

Small boards.

Reachable boards.

Places to put one hand or one foot when the dark made the whole crossing impossible to imagine.

The bridge is not finished.

I do not want to pretend it is.

There may still be wide gaps. There may still be places where the fog is thick and the water below sounds too loud. There may be boards that wobble. There may be days when you cannot step onto any of them.

But the bridge has boards now.

That matters.

You have language you did not have before.

When the light hurts, you can call it a splinter instead of a punishment.

When the thought sounds like truth, you can say:

The voice.

When the whole day is impossible, you can send one signal.

When the moment floods you, you can take one breath and step back.

When the world is too much, you can go to the room inside you, or touch the blanket if the room will not come.

When a good day arrives, you can let it be just today.

When a tool fails, you can try softer.

When something small reaches you, you can name a little color.

These are not victories you have to display.

They are handles.

They are boards.

They are ways to stay with yourself for one more moment.

Imperfect Still Counts

You may have used these tools imperfectly.

Good.

That means you used them as a human being.

Maybe you noticed the splinter of light only after it had already hurt you.

Maybe the voice had been talking for hours before you remembered to name it.

Maybe One Clean Signal was not a shower, but only putting one hand under water.

Maybe Breath and Step Back became only breath, or only step back, or only the wish to step back.

Maybe your safe room would not appear.

Maybe Just today was too large, so you had to shrink it to this minute.

Maybe Try softer sounded good on the page and impossible in your body.

Maybe a little color came and went so quickly you doubted it ever happened.

All of that counts.

Not because it looked clean.

Not because it produced a measurable outcome.

Not because you did it the way someone else might have done it.

It counts because you reached.

Even if you reached badly.

Even if you reached late.

Even if you reached and felt nothing.

Even if the only thing you did was read the words and think:

I cannot do this.

There is a kind of reaching that happens before action.

It is the tiny inward movement of not turning away completely.

It is the part of you that kept reading. The part of you that let one sentence sit near you. The part of you that did not slam the door on the possibility that one small thing might help someday.

That part may be very tired.

But it is still here.

And that matters.

If Still Here Feels Fragile

I want to be careful with this chapter because the phrase still here can land in different ways.

For some readers, it may feel grounding.

For others, it may feel fragile.

If still here feels fragile for you, if the gap between thinking about leaving and acting on that thought has become thin, if you are afraid of what you might do, or if you do not trust yourself to stay alive, please do not keep that alone.

This is not the moment to prove that you can use a tool privately.

This is the moment to let another human being become the tool.

Call or text 988 if you are in the United States.

If 988 is not available where you are, contact your local emergency number, crisis line, therapist, doctor, or a safe person who can physically be with you or help you get immediate support.

You do not have to explain the whole story.

You do not have to sound calm.

You do not have to make your pain understandable enough to deserve help.

You can say:

I do not trust myself to stay alive.

You can say:

I need someone with me.

You can say:

Please help me get through tonight.

That is not failure.

That is using the right tool for the level of danger.

If the house is on fire, you do not criticize yourself for not using a candle.

You call for help.

Your life is worth that call.

Your life is worth the interruption.

Your life is worth someone being inconvenienced, awakened, concerned, or brought closer.

You do not have to earn emergency care by being articulate, certain, polite, or easy to help.

Still here can be protected.

Let it be protected.

The Quiet Work of Staying

If you are not in immediate danger, but you are tired in the long, old way, this chapter is not asking you to make a speech about your future.

It is asking for something smaller.

Stay near yourself.

Not perfectly.

Not brightly.

Near.

When you notice the voice, stay near yourself by naming it.

The voice.

When your body feels like concrete, stay near yourself by making the next thing small enough to touch.

One signal.

When the day gets too large, stay near yourself by shrinking the frame.

Just today.

This hour.

This minute.

This breath.

When the tool fails, stay near yourself by refusing to turn on yourself.

Try softer.

When something gentle reaches you, stay near yourself by letting it be small.

A little color.

This is the quiet work of staying.

It is not glamorous.

It may not look like much from the outside.

But from inside the dark, it is enormous.

Every time you do not make your pain into a verdict against your worth, you are placing another board on the bridge.

Every time you let a small thing be small, you are placing another board.

Every time you ask for help instead of disappearing alone, you are placing another board.

Every time you survive a night you were not sure you could survive, even if you wake up exhausted and angry and unimpressed, another board is there.

The bridge may still be narrow.

It may still be incomplete.

But it is no longer nothing.

The bridge has boards now.

A board under your foot.

Not enough to make you fearless.

Not enough to make the crossing easy.

Enough to remind you that there is a place to stand while you decide the next small thing.

The Tools Can Stay Small

It may help to know that these tools do not expire when the book closes.

They do not become bigger because you have reached the last chapter.

They do not become obligations.

You are not now responsible for using all of them every day. You are not behind if you forget one. You are not failing the book if, tomorrow, the only words you remember are still here.

That may be enough.

The tools can stay small because the dark often makes everything too large. A whole recovery plan may feel impossible. A whole morning may feel impossible. A whole conversation may feel impossible. But a tiny handle can sometimes fit inside a hard minute.

Splinter can be enough when the light hurts.

The voice can be enough when a thought starts pretending to be truth.

One signal can be enough when your body cannot manage the bigger version of care.

One breath can be enough when the wave rises.

Safe room can be enough when the world outside you feels too sharp.

Just today can be enough when tomorrow feels like a cliff.

Try softer can be enough when effort turns against you.

A little color can be enough when one small thing reaches you through the gray.

Still here can be enough when you cannot find any other sentence.

Enough does not mean everything is fine.

Enough means there is one handle within reach.

If you use a handle and still feel terrible, the handle has not betrayed you. It may only have done the small job it was built to do.

A handrail does not move the whole staircase.

It gives your hand somewhere to go while your legs remember how to take the next step.

That is the scale we are keeping.

Small enough to use.

Kind enough to return to.

Honest enough not to promise what it cannot give.

That is why small can be trusted here.

It does not pretend to be more than it is.

You Do Not Have to See the Whole Way

One of the cruelest demands people make of someone in the dark is asking them to imagine a whole future.

What do you want your life to look like?

Where do you see yourself in five years?

What are you looking forward to?

Those questions may be loving in another season.

Here, they can feel impossible.

When you are fighting to survive the next ten minutes, five years is not a vision.

It is a wall.

So we are not asking for five years.

We are not even asking for five days.

We are asking for the next reachable light.

One candle.

One window.

One board.

One breath.

The light you can reach does not have to be the light that explains your whole life.

It only has to be enough light for the next step.

Sometimes that step is calling someone.

Sometimes it is drinking water.

Sometimes it is touching the blanket.

Sometimes it is putting the dangerous thing farther away from you.

Sometimes it is staying in the room with another person until the wave passes.

Sometimes it is closing the book and resting.

Sometimes it is reading one more sentence because one more sentence is all you can do.

The future can stay blurry.

You can stay here anyway.

You do not have to see the whole way in order to take the next small step.

You do not have to believe in morning in order to wait with someone until morning comes.

You do not have to feel hopeful in order to be held by a hope larger than what you can feel right now.

A Soft Blessing for the Bridge

If I could leave one thing beside you, it would not be a command.

It would not be a plan.

It would not be a bright speech about how everything happens for a reason.

It would be something quieter.

A small candle on the floor.

A blanket within reach.

A glass of water on the table.

A door that does not lock you in.

A window that can open when you are ready.

A board under your foot.

A voice beside you saying:

I am not leaving just because this is hard.

That is what this book has been trying to be.

Not the sun.

Not a cure.

Not a judge.

Not another person standing over you with a stopwatch, waiting to see whether you are improving fast enough.

A small light within reach.

A board on the bridge.

A way to remember, when the dark speaks in your own voice, that the dark is not the only voice in the room.

You are still here.

That may not feel like enough.

But it is not nothing.

It is a beginning that can begin again many times.

It is a fact the dark has not erased.

It is a place to put your hand.

Still here.

Still breathing, even if barely.

Still worthy, even if unconvinced.

Still allowed to need help.

Still allowed to rest.

Still allowed to try softer.

Still allowed to notice a little color.

Still allowed to take the next breath without knowing what comes after it.

For Today

For today, you do not have to feel triumphant about surviving.

You do not have to call yourself brave if that word feels too far away.

You do not have to turn your pain into a lesson, a testimony, a victory speech, or a plan.

You can begin with the smallest true sentence.

Still here.

If that sentence feels steady, let it be steady.

If that sentence feels fragile, let someone safe know.

If you do not trust yourself to stay alive, call or text 988 if you are in the United States. If you are somewhere else, contact your local emergency number, crisis line, or a safe person who can be with you now.

You are not failing by needing another human being.

You are using the right tool for the level of danger.

If the day is too large, shrink it.

Just today.

This hour.

This minute.

This breath.

If the voice gets loud, name it.

The voice.

If the tool fails, try softer.

If one small thing reaches you, let it be a little color.

If all you can do is keep your hand on the next board of the bridge, that counts.

You are still here, and that matters.

Still here.

Appendix: When the Dark Is Too Heavy

There will be days when the dark is too heavy to carry with a tool.

There will be days when the voice is too loud, when the gap between hearing it and believing it gets thin, when the bridge feels far away, when even the smallest version of the practice feels out of reach.

When that happens, you are not failing this book.

You are not failing recovery.

You are not failing at being strong enough.

You are receiving information.

The information is this: **this moment needs another human being.**

A book can keep you company.

A book can give you a sentence.

A book can remind you that the voice is not the only voice in the room.

But a book cannot sit beside you in an emergency. A book cannot drive you to care. A book cannot stay on the phone while the worst minute passes. A book cannot look into your face and help you choose the next breath.

When the dark is too heavy, please do not try to carry it alone.

You do not have to explain your entire life.

You do not have to make your pain sound reasonable.

You do not have to prove that you are in enough danger to deserve help.

You only have to say enough to let someone stand between you and the dark for this moment.

You can say:

I do not trust myself to stay alive.

You can say:

I might hurt myself if I am alone.

You can say:

I need someone to stay with me right now.

You can say:

The voice is too loud and I need help.

That is not weakness.

That is using the right tool for the level of danger.

If You Are in the United States

If you are in immediate danger, or if you may hurt yourself, call or text **988** to reach the Suicide & Crisis Lifeline. You can also use **988** chat through the official Lifeline website.

The **988** Lifeline is for mental health struggles, emotional distress, substance use concerns, and moments when you need someone to talk to. It is available day and night.

If you need text support, you can also text **HOME** to **741741** to reach Crisis Text Line.

If you are a veteran, service member, or someone concerned about one, you can call **988**, then press **1**, or text **838255** to reach the Veterans Crisis Line.

If you are an LGBTQ+ young person in crisis, feeling lonely, or thinking about suicide, you can reach The Trevor Project for crisis support. Use the current contact options listed at **thetrevorproject.org/get-help**.

If you are in immediate physical danger, call emergency services or go to the nearest emergency room.

If You Are Outside the United States

If **988** is not available where you are, contact your local emergency number, crisis line, doctor, therapist, hospital, or a safe person who can physically be with you now.

You can also search for local crisis help through an international helpline directory such as **findahelpline.com** or the International Association for Suicide Prevention crisis-centre directory.

Do not wait until you have perfect words.

Do not wait until you are sure it is bad enough.

If you are afraid you might not stay, that is enough reason to reach.

A Small Script for Reaching Out

If you cannot think clearly, copy one of these sentences and send it to a person you trust:

I am not safe alone right now. Can you stay with me or help me get support?

I do not need advice. I need you to sit with me until this passes.

I am scared of what I might do. Please call me now.

Can you help me call 988 or get to emergency care?

You are not being dramatic.

You are not being a burden.

You are letting the bridge hold more than one person.

That is what bridges are for.

Also by Angie G. Ford

The Splinter of Light Series

When the Light Hurts

A Quiet Companion for the Darkest Days of Depression

The Light You Can Reach

Practical Tools for Building a Bridge Out of the Dark

Holding the Light

How to Support Someone with Depression Without Losing Yourself

Coming soon.

The Done List Series

The Done List

Ease Anxiety with Small Daily Wins

The Done List for Loved Ones

How to Support Someone with Anxiety Without Losing Yourself

Fiction

Are You There, God? It's Me, Peggy.

We Were Going to Be Great Mothers

Journals and Trackers

Sweat, Swear, Survive

A Menopause Symptom Tracker for Hot Flashes, Mood Swings, and WTF Moments

All titles available on Amazon.

About the Author

Angie G. Ford writes fiction and nonfiction for women who are living in the middle of things. Her work sits at the intersection of emotional honesty, humor, and the complicated, beautiful lives women actually build.

She is the author of **The Done List**, **The Done List for Loved Ones, We Were Going to Be Great Mothers**, **Are You There, God? It's Me, Peggy.**, and **Sweat, Swear, Survive**. She writes under the Sunflower Phoenix Publishing imprint, a name that carries its own promise: something worth reading can grow from the ground up, and a story told with honesty is always worth telling.

When the Light Hurts was her love letter to anyone who has ever felt like the darkness was permanent, and to the quiet, stubborn strength it takes just to keep breathing.

The Light You Can Reach continues that promise. It does not ask the reader to become the sun. It offers small tools, small boards, and small lights for the next inch of the bridge.

A Note for Support Groups and Therapy Settings

The Light You Can Reach was written for the person reading alone in the dark, but it can also be used in the light, with care.

This book is not a replacement for therapy, medical care, crisis support, or clinical treatment. It is a companion language and tool book. In a therapy group, support circle, peer discussion, or guided reading setting, its purpose is not to push anyone into performance. Its purpose is to give people small, ordinary ways to name what is happening and reach for one next inch.

The tools in this book should stay gentle.

No reader should be required to share more than they want to share.

No one should be praised for sounding hopeful if they are not hopeful.

No one should be corrected into gratitude.

If a discussion uncovers immediate danger, suicidal intent, or fear that someone cannot stay alive, pause the discussion and reach for real-time support. Use 988 in the United States, local emergency services, a crisis line, a qualified professional, or a safe person who can physically be with the person in danger.

A tool is not enough when the danger is immediate.

A person is the tool then.

Discussion Questions

These questions are invitations, not assignments. You do not have to answer every question. You do not have to share anything that feels too raw, too private, or too unfinished. In a group setting, it is always acceptable to pass.

1. The introduction says that Book 1 named the room, and Book 2 shows where the matches are. Was there anything in this book that helped you name something you had been carrying quietly?

2. In Chapter 1, The Splinter Pause gives language for the moment when light hurts because you are tender, not hopeless. Have you ever had a small moment of light feel painful instead of comforting?

3. Chapter 2 teaches the sentence, **That is the voice. I do not have to answer it yet.** What is one kind of sentence the dark tends to use? What might change if you called it "the voice" instead of immediately calling it truth?

4. Chapter 3 turns One Clean Signal into a tiny action that interrupts the static. What

is one clean signal that might be small enough for a low-energy day?

5. Chapter 4 teaches Breath and Step Back as a way to make a little room around overwhelm. Where in your life might one breath or one small step back give you even a little more space?

6. Chapter 5 describes building a safe room in your mind. What might belong in a safe room for you? What would you want to keep outside the door?

7. Chapter 6 reminds us that a good day is not a contract. Have you ever felt pressure after a better day, either from yourself or from someone else?

8. Chapter 7 says that when a tool fails, the next instruction is not **try harder**. It is **try softer**. What would trying softer look like in one real part of your life?

9. Chapter 8 talks about the slow return of color without forcing hope. Has anything small reached you lately, even for a second: a smell, sound, texture, color, taste, memory, or moment?

10. Chapter 9 closes with **Still here.** What does that phrase feel like today? It may feel steady, fragile, numb, resistant, comforting, or something else entirely.

11. Which tool from this book feels most reachable right now? Which one feels far away? What would the smallest possible version of that tool be?

12. If you were sitting beside someone else in the dark, how could you offer one of these tools without turning it into pressure?

Closing Note

- You do not have to leave this book as a changed person.

- You do not have to close the last page and feel triumphant.

- You do not have to turn your survival into a speech.

- If all this book did was help you find one small board, one small sentence, one small pause, one small breath, one small light within reach, that matters.

- The bridge can begin there.

- Still here.

- Still breathing, even if barely.

- Still allowed to need help.

- Still allowed to try softer.

- Still allowed to begin again with the smallest thing.

- That is enough for today.

NOTES

www.ingramcontent.com/pod-product-compliance
Lightning Source LLC
LaVergne TN
LVHW100303210926
848480LV00003B/1013
* 9 7 9 8 9 9 5 9 4 1 3 5 4 *